D1506481

Building
YOUR
WEALTH
Inside Corporate America

Financial Strategies for Today's Executive

BRIGHTWORTH

authorHOUSE®

AuthorHouse™
1663 Liberty Drive
Bloomington, IN 47403
www.authorhouse.com
Phone: 833-262-8899

© 2021 Brightworth. All rights reserved.

No part of this book may be reproduced, stored in a retrieval system, or transmitted by any means without the written permission of the author.

Published by AuthorHouse 04/28/2021

ISBN: 978-1-6655-1647-1 (sc)
ISBN: 978-1-6655-1645-7 (hc)
ISBN: 978-1-6655-1646-4 (e)

Library of Congress Control Number: 2021902667

Print information available on the last page.

Any people depicted in stock imagery provided by Getty Images are models, and such images are being used for illustrative purposes only. Certain stock imagery © Getty Images.

This book is printed on acid-free paper.

Because of the dynamic nature of the Internet, any web addresses or links contained in this book may have changed since publication and may no longer be valid. The views expressed in this work are solely those of the author and do not necessarily reflect the views of the publisher, and the publisher hereby disclaims any responsibility for them.

CONTENTS

PREFACE

Why You Should Take the Time
to Read This Book

You've got e-mails to read, texts to respond to, global travel, rush hour, kids' soccer games, a dog that needs a walk, bills to pay, and your spouse or partner wanting a date night. How in the world do you find time to build wealth and manage money?

By picking up this book, you likely have questions about your money that are unanswered, or you don't feel confident about what you are doing with your money. You know how important it is to maximize your wealth and minimize your money mistakes; you're simply not sure where to go for answers. We have answers for you. This book can help you get your finances on track without taking precious time away from your other priorities. If you know your finances are buttoned up, you can more easily focus on what matters the most to you in life and the people you are with each day.

We've been purposeful on the content and design of each chapter: they are easy to read, the big takeaways are highlighted, and we speak to you, the busy executive running at a fast pace in corporate America. Throughout each chapter, we've included client stories amassed over three decades to demonstrate what has worked and where we've seen clients make mistakes. The names and specific details are changed, but the lessons learned are real and apply to today's executive.

After investing a short amount of time to read this book, our hope is you finish the last chapter with more confidence and security about your financial future than you have right now. You didn't get to this point in your career by not being intentional. It's time to be intentional with your money. Read on for practical, easy-to-understand, solid money strategies for today's busy corporate executive.

Disclosure:

The information and planning strategies detailed in this book are based on sources believed to be factual and reliable and are subject to change based on changes to the prevailing tax laws. The examples discussed in this book are provided for educational and illustrative purposes only and are not intended to be legal, tax, or investment advice. Please consult with your financial advisor or a tax or legal professional for questions about your specific situation. Executives should also work with their company benefit departments to ensure they understand the specific benefit plans available to them.

CHAPTER 1

The Basics of Financial Planning
for Every Executive

Up until now, if someone asked you what you are doing to plan for your financial future, you may have answered, "Throwing money into my 401(k)." You've been watching the balance go up and down, but you don't truly know whether you are saving enough or investing the right way. At the same time you have bills to pay, the mortgage with a balance that never seems to go down, kids' college expenses to think about, and vacation budgets. Is what you are making and saving today enough for the long term?

The term "financial planning" can be nebulous to most people, and perhaps even you, if you have never participated in a financial planning experience. Perhaps you have financial pieces in play today, yet they may be sporadic and not coordinated. If you've never sat down to map out how all the pieces fit together, it's hard to envision what your financial future may hold. That's where the financial planning process comes into play—to document where you are today and put together a strategy to get you on the right path to financial success.

The financial planning process starts with getting together all your financial, tax, insurance, and legal documents. For many people, this can be the hardest part of the process and can take the most time. But once you've got everything documented together, it should be a breeze from there!

There are six steps involved in the financial planning process.

1. Assembling your team (if hiring professionals) and taking stock of your present financial circumstances,
2. Establishing your goals and objectives,
3. Identifying your various options and alternatives,
4. Evaluating your options,
5. Implementing the selected strategies, and
6. Continually monitoring and revising your plan as needed.[1]

If you decide to engage specialists to guide you through your financial journey, what follows is a list of professional advisors who are commonly part of the financial planning team.

- Wealth advisor
- Financial planner
- Accountant (CPA)
- Estate attorney
- Trust officer
- Insurance agent
- Banker

Depending upon the professional advisors you decide to engage, we've found it is most efficient to select one person or firm to serve as your primary advisor, or financial quarterback. The person selected to occupy this role can unlock numerous intangible benefits for you—continuous communication among you and your team of advisors, minimizing frustration and unintended consequences, and increased assurance that your best intentions are implemented. We'll discuss how to select the right advisor further in chapter 16.

The first step in the financial planning process also includes assessing where you are today. Gathering together information on your assets, debts, income, and expenses is the starting point. In addition, tax and legal documents such as your wills, tax returns, premarital agreements, and insurance policies should be pulled together. This step in the process can be the most time-consuming part, however it's one of the most important.

If you leave out an important data point such as an old pension plan you forgot about or the remaining mortgage on your parents' house you committed to paying off, it can result in sending you down the wrong path or giving you false conclusions.

The second step in the process is stating your goals. As with business, you should establish SMART goals with your personal finances. Your goals should be specific, measurable, achievable, relevant, and time bound. For example, if you are considering retirement, "one day" is not a time frame that can be planned for. "Retiring at age fifty-five from corporate America with $15,000 per month of after-tax income, assuming I never go back to work or work part-time, using a 3 percent inflation rate and a life expectancy of age ninety-five" is a better statement of your retirement goal. Because financial planning is a lifelong process, continuing to monitor your spending, your portfolio's growth net of withdrawals, and health and economic changes in retirement is necessary to ensure you can remain comfortably and confidently retired. Undoubtedly, you can begin to see the overlap and parallels between the steps of proper personal planning and the ongoing strategic planning that occurs within your own organization. By engaging in a thorough financial planning process, the likelihood of unintended consequences or mishaps decreases exponentially, your ability to meet and exceed your goals will increase, and you should be empowered to focus on what matters most to you.

Next, we move on to steps three through six, which require some background as to what goes into a financial plan.

What Does a Financial Plan Cover?
A financial plan will address important questions and goals, such as:

- Am I on track to meet all my financial goals?
- How much should I be saving each year for retirement, and in what types of accounts?
- What should I do today to ensure I have enough to pay for my children's college education?
- Should I pay off my mortgage early?

- What's the best strategy for exercising my stock options?
- How much in stocks versus bonds should I have in my investment portfolio?

This list is customized to you—any financial objectives or concerns you have should be covered in your financial plan. And to make the plan most effective, the agreed-upon recommendations should be implemented as soon as possible upon the completion of the plan. Putting the plan on a shelf to collect dust is a waste of time for all involved in the planning process.

What follows are the basic elements included in a personal financial plan.

Establishing a Spending and Savings Plan

There are only five uses of money: spending (on lifestyle), saving, paying debts, paying taxes, and giving it away.

If you don't have a handle on how much you put toward each use, start with constructing a budget. Look back through bank and credit card statements, pay attention to monthly bills for three to six months, review last year's tax return and your current paystub, and consider one-time annual expenses like property taxes, insurance premiums, vacations, or large gifts. After completing your budget and comparing inflows (income) versus outflows (expenses), the goal is to put the excess to work in savings accounts to fund your short- and long-term financial goals. If you put this "extra" to work over a long period of time, you can accumulate significant wealth in a painless way.

Client Story

Bill was a mid-level employee working at a Fortune 500 company and was one of a handful of employees entrusted with the company's most closely guarded intellectual property secrets. When we first met Bill, we asked him what he did at his company. His response was, "I can't tell you."

At age seven, before school, Bill began work at dawn, sweeping the floor of his father's corner grocery store six days per week. It was at this early age that Bill learned the benefits of discipline and hard work. And it was the lessons learned at this early age that propelled his net worth over his working years. He began his career immediately after graduating from college and worked there for over 40 years, traveling to locations all over the world. As his career progressed and his loyalty became obvious to the top executives in his department, he was soon one of the few people in the company who was privy to its most closely guarded secrets.

A diligent saver thanks to his father's mentoring, he contributed the maximum to his 401(k) plan as soon as he was eligible, and his company matched an additional 3 percent. His 401(k) plan grew to over $2 million once he retired. Add to that his stock options and outside savings, and his net worth easily topped $10 million plus. From the lessons learned from his father—to be debt-free, live below your means, and save diligently—Bill and his wife were able to live the dream during retirement, boating the Intercoastal Waterway and the rivers of the Eastern United States on their beloved yacht.

Building an Emergency Savings Fund

A general rule of thumb is to have between three to twelve months' worth of living expenses in a savings account. Single-income households may want to embrace the upper end of this suggested range. In addition, if you are concerned your job may be eliminated in the near term, or you work in an industry that is cyclical, target a twelve-month emergency reserve.

A solid cash savings fund will help eliminate much stress in times of transition or life's inevitable financial surprises.

Risk Management and Insurance Planning

Life does not come without risks, but you most certainly have some control over how much risk you are willing to embrace. You can self-insure some risks or take steps to potentially transfer some of the risk away through either prudent planning or purchasing insurance (e.g., life, disability, medical, long-term care, and property and casualty insurance). Insurance is specifically designed to share the expenses of high-cost risk events with others in your insurance pool. The financial planning process evaluates whether you have the right amount and type of insurance coverage and how much of your annual budget should be allocated to insurance coverage (i.e., whether you are paying too much for your insurance). More details will be covered in chapter 7.

Another type of common risk corporate executives face, which you can't purchase insurance to cover, is company and concentration risk. This is having too much of your personal assets tied to your employer's stock. And because your current living expenses and ability to save for the future are dependent upon the employer who is giving you a paycheck, executives need to be mindful of how much of their overall financial well-being is tied to a single company. We dive further into concentration risk in chapter 4.

Investment Management and Saving for the Future

Be sure you pay yourself first by saving early and often. For each dollar you earn that is not earmarked for taxes owed, debt payments, education funding, charitable gifts, and one-time purchases (i.e., weddings), you have an opportunity and responsibility to determine how to best allocate the contributions to one or more investment accounts for retirement.

There are no scholarships for retirement! According to the US Census Bureau, the average retirement age in the United States is approximately age sixty-three, and the average length of retirement is roughly eighteen years. It can be overwhelming to think that you must accumulate enough money to live more than 6,500 days while you are no longer collecting a steady paycheck! Your investment portfolio is your economic engine to help ensure you don't run out of money during your thousands of days in retirement.

There isn't necessarily a "correct way" to manage investments, and there is no such thing as the perfect investment. However, it is more important to recognize that investing involves risk and rewards. There are numerous investment vehicles that can be utilized to help you meet and exceed your goals. Before you can settle on an appropriate investment strategy, you should be very deliberate and work through a series of questions such as:

- What are your investment goals and expectations?
- Which investment vehicles are most appropriate for you?
- How much should you save on a monthly basis in order to accumulate enough wealth by the time you retire or send your children to college?
- How much market volatility can you tolerate, and will this allow you to reach your financial goals?
- Does income taxation have any impact on the portfolio's investment allocation or design?
- How much time do you have between today and when you will need to access the money?

Savings and investment questions are common prompts we see as the initial reason people reach out to a professional advisor. Investments are critically important to achieve your financial goals, yet they are one of several components that must be coordinated to put you on path to success. We'll look more closely at investment strategies in chapter 2.

Debt Management

It is important that you develop a sound debt repayment strategy because not all debt is created equal. Home mortgage can be "good debt," whereas running up credit card debt is often "bad debt." Also, the true cost of debt should be measured in before-tax dollars. For example, paying off $10,000 in credit card debt could require $15,000 of before-tax income to pay the balance due.

When used and managed appropriately, debt can be a tool to help build wealth. If you don't have confidence investing your money, you may be taking all your extra cashflow each month to pay down debt. We've seen clients have a paid-for house by the age of forty, yet they have only a few thousand dollars in an investment portfolio. You can't send your kids to college on the equity in your house, or buy groceries in retirement, unless you essentially turn the equity into debt again!

Consider the following helpful tips and strategies as you manage your cashflow and build your financial foundation. First, take full advantage of a low interest rate environment by refinancing higher interest rate debts. Interest rates fluctuate over time, so pay attention to opportunities to save on interest expense. Next, aggressively pay off any outstanding balances on credit cards with high interest rates. Once you have fully paid off a credit card, never put yourself in a position where you can't pay your balance each month. If you need to, cut up the credit card and move to a debit card lifestyle.

Be mindful that some debt is tax-advantaged (i.e., deductibility of interest paid) whereas other debt is not. One common question we hear is, "Is it better to invest my money to earn more in the stock market than paying down my mortgage?" The lower your mortgage interest rate is, the stronger this argument can be. However, keep in mind that the interest you are paying is a fixed expense and is guaranteed, but the returns you'll earn on your investments are not guaranteed. By paying down your mortgage, you know what return you're getting (the mortgage interest rate).

Finally, consider fixed debt with shorter amortization schedules (i.e., fifteen-year mortgage vs. thirty-year mortgage) because it often results in a lower interest rate. Try to minimize or zero out your debt by the time you approach retirement. Debt payments are fixed expenses, and in retirement you want fixed expenses to be as low as possible.

Taxes

Managing income taxes is critical to maximizing your wealth because the more you make, the more you want to keep. But the more you make, the higher your tax bill. As a W-2 employee, there are simply limited ways you can save taxes, and tax laws are ever evolving. We'll dive more into taxes and tax strategies in

> Hire a good accountant who understands the complexities of executive compensation.

chapter 5. One important comment on taxes to remember: Don't be penny wise and pound foolish. Hire a good accountant who understands the complexities of executive compensation. Even though most of your income falls on one tax form each year (form W-2), it doesn't mean your tax situation is simple or appropriate for you to manage yourself.

Estate Planning

Not having a will, or having a very outdated will, is very common for corporate executives. This is typically one of the top recommendations we provide to our new corporate executive clients as they go through the financial planning process: Get your estate plan in place and up to date. If you don't have a will, it can end up costing your family thousands of dollars more in legal fees, taxes, probate costs, and undue headaches compared to the small investment of hiring a good estate lawyer during your life.

There are three documents every adult needs.

- Will
- Financial Power of Attorney
- Healthcare Power of Attorney

These documents should be reviewed every three to five years or when there is a major life event such as birth of a child, death of a family member, relocation to a new state, or inheritance received. If you have a good set of legal documents in place, you likely don't need to change them every few years, but a change in the estate tax laws could dictate otherwise.

We'll share more estate planning tips and strategies in chapter 8.

Conclusion

Steps three through six of the financial planning process will be developed and completed once you run the numbers. This includes identifying your options, evaluating your options, making decisions and implementing recommendations, and reviewing your decisions. The upcoming chapters will allow you do tackle steps three through six by equipping you with more financial knowledge and insight. Knowing where you stand and what you need to do going forward with your money will help bring a greater degree of happiness, security, and confidence to your life.

Chapter Endnote

1   CFP Board. "The Financial Planning Process". 2020. https://www.letsmakeaplan.org/getting-ready/the-financial-planning-process.

CHAPTER 2

Managing and Maximizing Your 401(k) Plan

Client Story

Tom grew up on a small family farm in rural Alabama, living off the land and barely having enough to get by. His parents worked from sunup to sundown, and so did he. At age eighteen, in 1957 Tom moved to Atlanta and landed a job in the mailroom of one of the largest corporations in America. Knowing the importance of saving, he started contributing to his company's 401(k) plan as soon as he was eligible.

From the mailroom he was soon promoted to the computer room. Today we have smartphones, but the company computer back then was the size of a thirty-foot by thirty-foot room and easily cost more than $2 million. The computer code was input onto hundreds of three-inch by seven-inch punch cards. Tom's hard work paid off, and he rose to overseeing IT for the whole company by the late 1970s.

As he continued to excel at his work, he was granted stock options, an annual bonus, and a continually expanding salary. Did he spend the increase? No. Instead, he saved it, increasing his 401(k) plan contributions whenever he could. He later shared with us that he never looked at his statements—he simply put them unopened in a pile in his desk—until he was preparing for retirement thirty-five years later. Although we don't recommend ignoring your 401(k) balance, it's better than constantly fretting over it and making excessive changes every year.

When we first met with Tom in his office, he pulled out the stack of unopened quarterly statements. "What's that?" we asked. "These are my 401(k) plan statements; I've never looked at them." He then proceeded to open his latest statement, and his eyes got so wide that it looked like he had just seen a ghost. "Oh, my goodness!" Tom exclaimed. "My 401(k) is worth $1.5 million! I had no idea it was this big!"

He and his wife are now in their mid-eighties and are financially secure and living comfortably. The key to their success? Living a non-consumptive lifestyle, saving early, and remaining debt free.

> The key to their success? Living a non-consumptive lifestyle, saving early, and remaining debt free.

Funding Your 401(k)

All executives should be putting the maximum allowed annually into their 401(k) plan. Period. Maximum funding your 401(k) plan does not mean putting in the maximum amount your employer will match. It means deferring the amount of your paycheck allowed based on IRS limits. In 2021, people under age fifty can defer up to $19,500 into their 401(k), and those aged fifty and above can defer $26,000. This extra amount for those aged fifty and above is called a "catch-up contribution." These limits increase every year or two, so be sure to continually monitor your paycheck to make sure you are on track to max out each year. Because the deposits are made automatically from your paycheck into your 401(k), this account can build quickly. For most people, saving only in your 401(k) will not be enough to retire.

> Saving only in your 401(k) will not be enough to retire.

Pre-tax or Roth 401(k)?

Most 401(k) plans offer two types of accounts; a pre-tax (or before-tax) 401(k) and a Roth 401(k). The difference is whether you receive a tax deduction on your contributions, and how the money is taxed when it's withdrawn in retirement. For most executives, it makes sense to put your money into the pre-tax 401(k) to receive the tax deduction—one of the very few ways to save taxes each year. For example, your taxable income is $300,000 annually. A 401(k) deposit of $19,500 will save about $6,000 in income tax assuming your average annual federal and state tax rate combined is 30 percent. In retirement, when you withdraw money from your 401(k), you'll pay tax at that time and at your then current tax bracket, which is presumably lower than in your working years.

On the other hand, a Roth 401(k) can be the better choice for young executives who are just starting their careers and earning less than approximately $150,000, because they are in a lower tax bracket. Withdrawals from Roth 401(k) plans are tax-free in retirement (after age fifty-nine and a half) based on current tax law. Or, if you believe your tax rate will be higher in retirement (expecting a huge inheritance? moving to a higher tax rate state?), funding a Roth 401(k) and foregoing the tax deduction now may make sense.

A limited number of 401(k) plans offer a third type of account for which you can put money into, which is called an after-tax account. It is different than a Roth 401(k). Here, you can put money into the after-tax account on an after-tax basis like the Roth 401(k), the earnings grow tax-deferred like the pre-tax 401(k) and the Roth 401(k), and when you take withdrawals or rollover the after-tax account to an IRA at retirement, a portion of the withdrawal will be tax-free. If your employer offers this type of account within the 401(k) plan, it may be wise to put some money into it after maximum funding your pre-tax 401(k) account. Some 401(k) plans allow you to convert your after-tax account balance to a Roth 401(k) periodically throughout the year, which can be a good long-term tax move, but you may pay a small amount of tax each year on the portion of the conversion that equals earnings. Or when you leave your employer, you can rollover the after-tax contributions in the after-tax account to a Roth IRA and roll the earnings portion of the after-tax account (the part that's not yet been taxed) to a traditional IRA. Both of these rollovers will result in zero dollars in tax if handled properly.

There are special IRS limits for the amount you can put into the after-tax account as well, whereby the total of your employer match, your pre-tax or Roth 401(k) contributions, and your after-tax account contributions cannot exceed $58,000 in 2021 for those under age fifty, or $64,500 in 2021 for those aged fifty and above.

How to Invest Your 401(k)

This is one of the most common questions we get from our new executive clients. It makes sense because for many, it's the primary investment account into which they are putting money.

There is typically a list of funds you can choose to invest in, as well as your employer's stock (if you work for a publicly traded company). We have seen several people who were nowhere near the executive level invest 100 percent of their 401(k) in their company stock and retire with over $1 million in their 401(k). They got lucky. They bet the farm on their employer, and it worked out for them. But had their company not fared well during their working years, a long recession occurred, a bad leader was in place, there was a company scandal, or there was negative media exposure, the $1 million could have been worth pennies—and their job probably would have been eliminated if any of these issues had occurred.

Most publicly traded companies have the company 401(k) match invested in company stock as a default inside the 401(k) plan. You can sell that stock with no restrictions and no taxes, assuming you are not on a restricted trading list. Outside of the company match, be very thoughtful about how much of your own money you invest in company stock. Your dollars should be diversified among the list of funds offered in your plan. With investing, the majority of the investment return you'll earn over time is a result of your asset allocation—how much you have in stock and bonds—and not the specific stock, mutual fund, or bond you select. Those selections are important, but asset allocation plays a larger role.

Many 401(k) plans have online tools to help guide you in selecting a reasonable asset allocation given your age, but it's important to know this tool doesn't understand who you are, your goals, what other assets or income you will have in retirement—and it won't ping you when it's time to make a change to your investment mix. But outside of professional help, it's a decent starting point.

Here are some other investment guidelines for different age groups.

For those in their twenties, thirties, and early to mid-forties, having most of your 401(k) plan in stock funds is a good idea. US stocks as measured by the S&P 500 Index have averaged 13.8 percent annually over the last ten years (through December 31, 2020).[1] However, as you approach retirement, the amount of stocks or stock funds should be decreasing because your time frame for needing to spend that money is drawing near. You can't afford to withstand a sharp decline in your 401(k) account right before your planned retirement. Those in their fifties should consider having 20–40 percent of their 401(k) in bond funds.

Do not try to time the market with erratically moving around your 401(k) investments. It's rare that going all to cash is a good idea. Timing the market is impossible. If you happen to get more conservative before a stock market downturn, the odds are not in your favor to get back in at the right time before the market goes up. A better strategy is to reduce the amount of stocks or stock funds in your account if you are losing sleep at night over what may happen in the stock market, or you are nearing retirement and know you'll need to start living off this money soon. Otherwise, the best strategy for your 401(k) is to keep putting money into it, have a diversified strategy that is rebalanced at least annually, and don't watch it every day. See chapter 13 for a more detailed discussion regarding how to invest during a financial downturn.

What follows are sample investment allocations for your 401(k) account based on age. A very important note: This is not specific investment advice but rather a general guideline for how much to invest in stocks or bonds during your career. These percentages could easily adjust 10–20 percent or more based on your circumstances or market conditions.

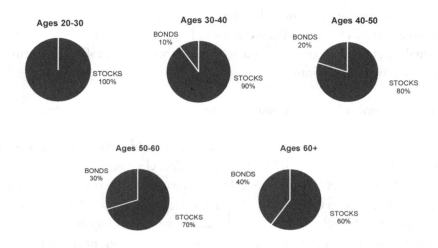

Taking Out a Loan on Your 401(k)

Don't do it. If you have planned well and built and emergency fund (cash savings), you should hopefully avoid running into a bind and needing a personal loan. Even though loans are allowed against a 401(k) account, it doesn't mean you should act on it. Typically, you will have put before-tax dollars into your 401(k), only to have to pay the loan back with after-tax dollars. This results in losing a major tax advantage of your 401(k). If you leave your company, you must pay back this loan quickly; company plan rules will dictate the timing, such as within ninety days of departure. That alone can put you in another financial bind.

Should I Roll Over My 401(k) to an IRA?

We typically recommend taking your 401(k) with you when you leave your employer. All too often we see executives who have jumped from company to company and end up with forgotten retirement accounts that have been neglected. You work hard to save this money, so why not keep track of it?

In an IRA, you have essentially an unlimited list of investments to choose from, whereas your employer (or former employer) has a limited list available in the 401(k) plan. If you choose to have a professional manage your IRA, you'll pay them a fee. This management fee does not exist if you leave your 401(k) at your employer; it's then up to you to manage your money. Nobody at your former company will pay attention to your 401(k) account, including those reachable on an 800 line who can't give investment or tax advice.

If you leave your company at age fifty-five or later, but you are not yet age fifty-nine and a half, it may make sense to leave a portion of your 401(k) account at your former company. The reason is there is a special tax rule that allows you to take a withdrawal from the 401(k) account without incurring the 10 percent early retirement withdrawal tax penalty that would occur for balances withdrawn out of an IRA before age fifty-nine and a half. Regardless of whether your retirement savings is in a 401(k) account or an IRA, withdrawals must begin by age seventy-two, in the amount of approximately 4 percent annually. There is an IRS table that dictates the percentage that must be withdrawn at each age beginning at age seventy-two, and that percentage increases as you age.

Net Unrealized Appreciation

Here are two questions before reading this next section:

1. Do you own employer stock in your 401(k)?
2. Has it doubled or tripled in value?

If you answered yes to these two questions, then this section is for you.

There is a special provision in the tax code that allows people leaving their company to take an in-kind distribution of company stock from their 401(k) plan and only pay income tax on the cost basis of the shares

> 1. Do you own employer stock in your 401(k)?
>
> 2. Has it doubled or tripled in value?

(subject to certain restrictions). It's called the Net Unrealized Appreciation, or NUA strategy.

Let's look at an example. Rick was in middle management and had worked at a public company for over forty years. When he was hired at age twenty-three, he started socking away as much money as he could into the company 401(k) plan, investing exclusively in his company's stock. Little did he know that his plan would grow to over $4 million by the time he would retire.

When we first met with Rick, we asked him to request a "hypothetical in-kind distribution estimate" from the 401(k) plan provider. This is a document that shows what he paid for the company stock over the years, also known as his cost basis. In addition, it shows how much was contributed to the plan both before-tax and after-tax over the years. Rick had significant appreciation in his shares, resulting in a cost basis of only $800,000. And because he had saved considerably in addition to his 401(k)—he received grants of stock options each year—here's what Rick was able to do when he retired:

Rick decided to keep $1 million of company stock and roll $3 million of his 401(k) tax-free to an IRA. He diversified his IRA into a balanced portfolio of stocks and bonds, and because he didn't need the money to live on, he allowed his IRA to grow tax-deferred until required distributions were to begin at his age seventy and a half (now age seventy-two).

He took the $1 million of company stock and deposited it into a brokerage account. The good news here is that he had to pay income tax only on the cost basis—$200,000 in this example.

Then because Rick was charitably inclined, he contributed $500,000 of his stock to a donor-advised fund (discussed further in chapter 5), resulting in a charitable deduction of $500,000. The net tax savings to Rick totaled $105,000 ($500,000 charitable contribution, minus $200,000 taxable income resulting from the in-kind distribution, multiplied by a 35 percent income tax rate equals $105,000).

Indeed, NUA is a great technique to use for those special situations for employees with a very low-cost basis in their company shares within their

401(k) plan. In the situation where the employee has a charitable intent for some of those shares, NUA can be a great technique to consider.

Important note: *NUA is a very technical area of the Internal Revenue Code, and there are only a limited number of advisors with adequate knowledge in this area. If you think NUA might work for you, make sure you consult an expert who can guide you and assist in avoiding the many landmines surrounding NUA.*

Chapter Endnote

1   Past performance is not a guarantee of future investment returns. Investors cannot invest directly in an unmanaged index. Provided for illustrative purposes only.

CHAPTER 3

Deferred Compensation Plans

Highly compensated executives may have access to retirement savings accounts that only a select number of people in the organization do. One example is a nonqualified deferred compensation plan.

First, a Word of Caution

Deferred compensation plans are essentially an IOU from the employer to the employee, to pay funds in the future. Once you defer money into this plan, you become a creditor of your company. Unlike 401(k) plans, deferred compensation plans are not covered under the protections of the Employee Retirement Income Security Act (ERISA). If your company goes bankrupt, these nonqualified plans are considered unsecured debt of the company, and you may never see your money. You do not get preferential treatment simply because you are or were an employee.

After filing for bankruptcy in 2012, Eastman Kodak's settlement included only paying 4–5 percent of an executive's deferred compensation account balance out to the executive. Through GM's bankruptcy proceedings, executives lost about two-thirds of their deferred compensation account balances that were in excess of $100,000.

If you are concerned about the financial health of your employer, you may want to pass on the opportunity to participate in the deferred compensation plan. We recommend you maximum fund your 401(k) plan first before deferring money into a nonqualified deferred compensation plan.

Saving into a Deferred Compensation Account

Deferred compensation plans allow the participant to defer salary or bonus today, invest the funds in a tax-deferred account, and set up a schedule to withdraw the money at some point in the future. By choosing not to receive your income in the current year, you do not have to pay federal and state income taxes on that portion of your compensation in the year of deferral.

For example, you earn $400,000 annually and are forty-five years old. If you are only setting aside money into the company's 401(k) plan, you are saving less than 5 percent of your income on a pre-tax basis ($19,500 / $400,000 = 4.875%). That's a tax savings of about $6,825 assuming your federal and state tax rate is 35 percent. Conversely, if you elect to defer 10 percent of your earnings into the deferred compensation plan, coupled with the 401(k), you are now saving $59,500 annually, or nearly 15 percent of your income. That's a much better savings percentage as it relates to retirement planning. Plus, you've now saved over $20,000 in tax.

Like your 401(k), most deferred compensation plans offer a lineup of funds to choose from when investing your money. The more investment options that are available, the easier it will be to allocate the funds in a diversified strategy that is appropriate for your specific time horizon. Like all investment decisions, you'll also need to consider your risk appetite and potential market risk. It's best to avoid putting too much of your deferred income in company stock if that is an investment option inside your deferred compensation plan.

Taking Your Money Out

Although 401(k) distributions can generally be taken at any time in retirement, deferred compensation participants must elect a distribution period at the time of deferral. Most plans allow for either a lump sum payment in a specific calendar year or upon your retirement, or equal payments over a period of years at retirement. In most cases, you'll want to take your distributions during retirement when other income sources are likely to be less than during your working years, and you need the cash flow. Also, it usually makes sense to spread your distributions over several years versus electing a lump sum payment.

Electing annual payments may be beneficial for several reasons. First, it allows the funds to stay invested in the deferred compensation plan longer, creating an opportunity for more years of tax-deferred growth. Second, it should help smooth out your annual income during the distribution period because you are receiving the funds in equal payments over five, ten, or fifteen years. If you choose a lump sum at retirement, the tax-deferred funds will be paid in a single tax year, resulting in a very large tax bill.

Deciding how long of a distribution period may depend on several factors, including your anticipated retirement age and the age you plan to commence Social Security. For example, if you plan to retire at age sixty, it may make sense to choose a distribution period of ten to fifteen years upon retirement. Depending on the amount you've accumulated in the deferred compensation plan, these distributions may help bridge the gap between your retirement and the time you are subject to required minimum distributions from your IRA (currently age seventy-two). These payments may also allow you to defer commencing Social Security in order to take advantage of the 8 percent annualized increase in Social Security benefits from your "full retirement age" to age seventy.

Also, though it is difficult to project future income tax rates, the goal is (1) your current tax rate will be lowered today by deferring the income in your prime working years, and (2) your taxable income in retirement will also be lower than it is today when the deferred compensation distributions are paid out.

We find many executives have scattered payout elections, and there is no rhyme or reason as to why they chose a lump sum payout for one plan year, five years for another, and ten-year payouts for other plans years. Stay on top of your payout elections and review them each year. It's best to have a coordinated payout plan that works with your other retirement income sources, which can dictate changing your previous payout elections. This can sometimes be difficult, come with strings attached, or not be allowed. Let's say you elected the lump sum payout option for plan year 2010, but you've changed your mind and now want that money to pay over ten years in retirement. If the plan year you want to change is 2004 or later, and changes are allowed by your plan, based on tax law there is a five-year waiting period you must meet before the funds can begin to pay. This means the first year in retirement that the 2010 plan year's annual payments can begin is year six of retirement.

Finally, your retirement distribution election could very well take effect when you leave your company but don't actually retire. Perhaps you leave your employer to work elsewhere. Depending upon your plan's rules, your retirement payment elections could immediately begin, and the cash starts paying out. Or in some cases, you may have elected a ten-year retirement payment, but based on plan rules, a default lump sum election happens if you were to quit your job before a certain age.

Choosing the best distribution period during the enrollment period is one of the most important decisions to make when participating in these types of plans. Be sure to understand the nuances of the plan's payout rules, especially if you leave your company to work someplace else.

CHAPTER 4

Equity Awards—Stock Options, Restricted Stock, Performance-Based Stock

Executives' stock awards can become the sole reason they are able to retire comfortably—or not. They can become the largest asset on the balance sheet. Pay careful attention to this chapter.

Executive compensation packages are often much more complicated than the usual base salary and annual bonus. Good companies want to attract and retain valuable talent. Granting equity awards is a way to motivate employees to work hard to increase the value of the company and its stock price. Equity awards can help you participate in your company's growth, build wealth, pay for your kids' education, and retire when you want. But you must make wise decisions with your equity.

> Executives' stock awards can become the sole reason they are able to retire comfortably—or not. They can become the largest asset on the balance sheet. Pay careful attention to this chapter.

Although executives can benefit greatly from receiving equity awards, the drawbacks are they don't feel they have the time to keep track of the equity awards, they do not fully understand the tax implications, and they often find themselves overexposed to their company stock.

Client Story

Sam first met with us in 2006 when the stock market was on fire, reaching new heights almost every week. He was a stuffy, stodgy corporate lawyer. His plans were to retire within the next five years. After counseling hundreds of corporate executives over the years, we figured his income was over $250,000 and that he had a truckload of stock options. Our income assumptions were correct, but we were off on the number of stock options he had.

He shared with us, "Every time one of my stock option grants reaches the 100 percent vesting stage, we cash it in and build onto our barn, buy more horses, or pay down a small amount of debt. And because our company stock continues to perform, we can't go wrong with this strategy. After all, our stock never goes down in value." Red flag: *past performance is not a guarantee of future performance.*

Red flag: *past performance is not a guarantee of future performance.*

We did not engage Sam as a client, but we did learn later that his stock options quickly became worthless. His company started restructuring with involuntary terminations and downsizing. He was one of the first to go. So much for job security.

This is an example of what can go wrong with a lackluster stock option strategy. Having a formal, written financial plan, knowing the goals you are working toward, and understanding what your personal finish line looks like allows you to make better decisions regarding what to do with your company stock awards. We have seen many clients make wise decisions with their stock options, and doing it with confidence, when we have a roadmap to reference back to.

> Having a formal, written financial plan, knowing the goals you are working toward, and understanding what your personal finish line looks like allows you to make better decisions regarding what to do with your company stock awards.

In this chapter, we outline the most common forms of equity awards, discuss more pitfalls to avoid, and provide recommendations on maximizing your awards' after-tax value.

Stock Options—The Big Picture

Stock options are essentially the right to purchase a certain number of shares of your company's stock, at a specified price, over a defined period. For example, you may be granted one thousand stock options with a grant price of $10 per share. One-half of the options (or five hundred shares) may vest next year, and the remainder vest the year following. Once vested, you may have ten years to exercise until the options expire. This is a basic structure, but it's simply an example, and each company's options will work a little differently.

The gap between the price you exercise at and the price the stock is trading at when you exercise is the value of the option and is taxable as income. For example, you are granted one thousand stock options when the stock is trading at $10 per share, the stock price grows, and you exercise them at $25 per share. The value of the option upon exercise is $15 per share, or $15,000 in this example. That is the amount on which you pay tax. It often makes sense to spread out exercising stock options over several taxable years to help smooth out your income and potentially stay out of the top income tax bracket.

Executives at publicly traded companies who are on a restricted trading list will be able to exercise and sell options only during an open trading window. If offered by your company, setting a Rule 10b5-1 Stock Trading Plan is often a good strategy that allows you to systematically exercise and sell shares even during closed trading windows. More on this later.

It's important to remember stock options have expiration dates. You do not want to miss deadlines and have valuable options expire. It's also important to look at the value of your options in the context of your overall financial picture. Concentration in your company stock can build tremendous wealth if the company performs well, but it can also hinder your lifestyle if the stock heads in the wrong direction. After all, if your company struggles, it can affect your stock options, your cash compensation, and your job security.

Two Types of Stock Options—NSOs and ISOs

There are two types of stock options: Incentive stock options (ISOs) and nonqualified stock options (NSOs or NQSOs). They are treated differently for income tax purposes.

Nonqualified Stock Options (NSOs)

Most public companies today issue NSOs. Over the past several years, we've seen some companies switch entirely away from issuing any type of stock option in favor of restricted stock, which we'll discuss later in this chapter.

To determine whether your stock option is an NSO, look at the option agreement. If tax withholding is required upon exercise, then you know it's an NSO. As mentioned above, the gap between the price you exercise at and the price the stock is trading at when you exercise is the value of the option, and with NSOs it is taxed as ordinary income. Federal, state (if applicable), Medicare, and Social Security taxes will be withheld upon exercise. The maximum federal ordinary income rate is 37 percent (as of January 2021). When you add in state, Medicare, and Social Security taxes, the total tax rate could get up to 45–50 percent. Many companies will allow you to withhold some of the shares you are exercising to cover the tax withholding amount. Unfortunately, this withholding is typically too low, and you'll want to make sure you have adequate cash on hand to cover any additional taxes due from exercising the options.

Incentive Stock Options (ISOs)

Many privately held companies and start-ups issue ISOs. ISOs receive special tax treatment and are exempt from immediate ordinary income tax upon exercise. However, exercising an ISO is subject to Alternative Minimum Tax (AMT). The maximum AMT tax rate is 28 percent for federal tax (as of January 2021), plus there will be state income tax. You pay the AMT tax when you file your tax return.

ISOs remain as ISOs only while you are employed at your company, and they cannot be extended beyond ninety days after you leave. ISOs typically convert to NSOs after ninety days of termination of employment. (NSOs don't require employment and can be extended well beyond ninety days).

As with NSOs, the gap between the price you exercise at and the price the stock is valued at when you exercise is the value of the option. This spread is reportable as AMT income on your tax return. Assume you are granted one thousand incentive stock options when the stock is valued at $10 per share, the stock price grows, and you exercise them at $25 per share. The value of the incentive stock option upon exercise is $15 per share, or $15,000. That spread is the amount you report on your tax return on Form 6251. Your cost basis for purposes of selling the net shares you receive from the exercise is a little tricky. For regular tax purposes, your cost basis is the exercise price of the option ($10 per share). For AMT purposes, the cost basis is the fair market value upon exercise ($25 per share). If you wait at least one year to sell the net shares you received from this stock option exercise, the gain will be taxed at favorable long-term capital gains tax rates.

If an ISO is sold within one year of the exercise or within two years of the grant date, then a "disqualifying disposition" occurs. In this case, taxation of the ISO works more like taxation of an NSO. The spread between the exercise price and the fair market value (FMV) will be taxed as ordinary income, and the spread between the FMV and the final sale price is taxed as a short-term capital gain or loss. However, the ISO income from the disqualifying disposition isn't subject to Medicare or FICA tax. Therefore, a disqualifying disposition from the exercise and sale of an ISO can be less expensive than the ordinary income taxes paid on exercising an NSO.

If you have ISOs, you will want to consult with a tax professional to make sure you understand the special tax nuances.

Stock Option Exercise Strategies

One of the most common questions we hear from our executive clients is, "What is the best strategy for exercising my stock options?" This can be the million-dollar question!

Generally speaking, waiting until closer to the expiration date of the stock option is best, even if the stock rises in value a small amount each year. Let's look at an example.

You are granted a nonqualified stock option to purchase ten thousand shares at an exercise price of $50 per share in 2021. This option expires in 2031. At issuance the stock is trading at $50. The grant vests 25 percent per year over four years. Let's say the stock price rises by 3 percent per year during this ten-year period. If you exercise in year five, your gain—the value you receive from this grant—is approximately $80,000 (the stock is now trading in year five at $58 per share). However, if you wait until year ten to exercise your option, right before expiration of the option, the value you receive is $172,000. That's more than a 200 percent increase in the value of the option in that last five years, whereas the price of the stock only increased by 16 percent. This is the leverage you get from stock options.

We've seen plenty of executives exercise their stock options annually as they vest. As you can see from the above example, that can be a costly maneuver. However, if the stock price declines over time, exercising as soon as possible can be the smartest move. The stock option can also be worthless if the stock declines below the grant or exercise price ($50 in the above example). This is the big risk with stock options!

Typically, executives will have a good sense of the future direction and profitability potential of their company because they are involved in the inner workings day-to-day, whereas Wall Street analysts are not. That's why we like to ask our executive clients their opinion of the stock, because sometimes it's contrary to analysts' opinions.

Nobody has a crystal ball when it comes to predicting stock prices or stock returns, so it's best to run the numbers to understand what stock price you need to exercise each grant at in order to achieve your financial goals. For example, if the stock price reaches $55 per share, and you exercise all your options, does that mean you'll then have enough money to retire, send your kids to college, or buy a vacation home? Conversely, if the stock price drops to $45 per share, does that mean you are no longer on track to meet your goals and would have to work longer, spend less in retirement, or take out loans to pay for your children's college? Knowing at what stock price you need to exercise your stock options to achieve your personal financial goals is the best strategy for determining when to push the sell button.

> Knowing at what stock price you need to exercise your stock options to achieve your personal financial goals is the best strategy for determining when to push the sell button.

If you work for a publicly traded company and are on the restricted trading list, you don't have the flexibility to exercise whenever you want or when the stock reaches your magic price target. If your company offers a 10b5-1 stock trading plan, take advantage of it. You establish a stock trading plan during an open trading window, set a price at which you want your stock option grant(s) exercised, set the time frame for the plan to stay in place (six months, one year, etc.), and then wait. The beauty of these plans is that your stock option can get exercised during a closed window without running afoul of the insider trading rules. You will hop, skip, and jump down the hallway the first time you experience being able to take advantage of a daily upswing in the stock price during a closed trading window!

When exercising stock options, you typically have the choice to receive the value in cash or shares of company stock. For many of our clients, unless they have a stock ownership requirement not yet met, we recommend the "cashless sale" strategy whereby they receive cash for the value of their options upon exercise. This is a way to systematically diversify your stock concentration. You're likely getting new stock awards each year, so even when you do a cashless exercise during your working years, you may find you still own the same percentage of company stock in your total portfolio. Another option is a cashless hold strategy, where you receive the net value of the stock option in shares of company stock.

What do you do with the stock option proceeds, especially if you choose the cashless sale option? First, set aside some of the cash to cover extra taxes due when you file your tax return, because the amount of tax withheld is often not enough given your tax bracket. (This is the case even if you do a cashless hold). Next, allocate the cash toward meeting your goals. Pay down your mortgage, save in your children's college 529 plan accounts, put money in an IRA or taxable brokerage account for retirement, and give some to charity or other impactful uses. Don't use the money to constantly pay off credit card debt, put a big pool in the backyard, go on lavish vacations, or pay for private K–12 expenses. If you find you are a culprit of doing just that, you are spending too much money on your lifestyle and need to cut back. If you get too comfortable having stock options bail you out of poor spending decisions, one day you could be in big trouble if your company stock underperforms, a recession comes, you lose your job and can't get a new one with the same level of stock grants, or bad vibes hit the news and social media about your company, and it eventually goes under.

> As the famous Kenny Rogers song goes, with stock options, the key is to "know when to hold 'em and know when to fold 'em."

As the famous Kenny Rogers song goes, with stock options, the key is to "know when to hold 'em and know when to fold 'em."

Restricted Stock or Performance-Based Restricted Stock

Restricted stock, or performance-based restricted stock, is an increasingly common form of executive compensation. It's a long-term incentive vehicle. Some companies have done away with stock options and are issuing only restricted stock or performance-based stock in the long-term incentive plan. Restricted stock is easier for most people to understand than stock options, which have more nuances and complexities. Unlike with stock options where you need to take action to exercise them, little to no action is required to receive shares of your company stock through a release of the restricted stock award.

With restricted stock, a target award is granted to the executive, and a future date is set for when the award will vest and pay out to the executive. Time is the main requirement that needs to be met in order to receive the shares from the restricted stock award. Once released, the value of the stock is taxable as ordinary income, and that income appears on your paystub. Often the company will withhold a set number of shares to cover the tax withholding requirements.

On the other hand, with performance-based restricted stock, the actual number of shares received is determined at the end of a performance period. The final award may be based on company performance, department performance, or even individual performance. After the performance period is met, the award may be released immediately, or it may be subject to a holding period. Once released, the value of the shares is taxable as ordinary income, and that income appears on your paystub. Again, employers often withhold some of the shares to help cover the tax liability.

As with stock options, it's unlikely the amount of taxes withheld upon the release of the award(s) will be enough, and you'll likely want to keep some cash set aside to cover the underwithholding when you file your income tax return for that year. This could mean selling some of the stock once it's released to you, so you have cash available.

If you receive a restricted stock award, you may have the option to file an 83(b) tax election. An 83(b) election is available for certain types of restricted stock and gives you the option of paying ordinary income tax based on the fair market value of the stock on the day it is granted, rather than recognizing the income when it vests. This election would allow the recipient to receive favorable capital gain tax treatment on any gains that arise after the grant date and 83(b) election. However, if the value of the stock goes down from the date of grant and the date of release, you will have overpaid tax by filing the 83(b) election, and you don't receive a refund of this overpayment.

The alternative to making an 83(b) election is to defer paying any tax until the stock is fully vested and released to you. If you choose this option and the stock has appreciated, then you end up paying ordinary income tax on a higher value because the stock is worth more when it vests, perhaps three or five years after the grant date. However, you don't risk overpaying tax for a stock that could be worth much less when you get control of it.

The released shares can be sold at any point in time (assuming you are not on the restricted trading list). Assuming an 83(b) tax election is not made, if you sell the shares immediately upon release, you are likely to owe very little, if any, capital gains taxes. If the released shares rise in value, and you sell them within twelve months of release, any gain after the release date will be taxable as a short-term capital gain at your top marginal tax bracket. That could mean around 40 percent or more in tax is due on the gain. If you don't sell the shares upon release, it often makes sense to hold them past twelve months to get the more favorable long-term capital gains tax treatment, which results in a lower tax rate. Like stock options, you need to have a plan for how to put the proceeds from the restricted stock awards to good use in order to achieve your long-term goals.

Stock options, restricted stock, and performance-based restricted stock can be extremely valuable assets for an executive and result in the difference between being financially secure long-term or not. Having a plan to capture the value from these awards is essential for any executive.

CHAPTER 5

Taxes

In addition to understanding how their compensation packages are taxed, it can also be difficult for executives to find ways to save taxes as compared to business owners or other self-employed workers. In this chapter, we will highlight some of the important tax considerations when dealing with executive compensation plans, and identify some ways to save taxes along the way.

Taxes 101

Individuals in the United States are cash basis taxpayers. This means that you report income in the year that you are actually paid. For your base salary, this is a relatively straightforward concept because you report the income in the year you receive your paycheck. Likewise, annual bonuses are reported in the year that your bonus is received.

Most executives will receive an IRS Form W-2 each year that reports annual income and tax withholding. When you first start with the company, you'll likely fill out the IRS Form W-4, where you determine the amount of federal taxes your employer will withhold from your paycheck. There will also be a similar form to elect state tax withholding, depending on your home state. We recommend consulting with an accountant when completing the W-4

> We recommend consulting with an accountant when completing the W-4 form because every taxpayer's situation is different.

form because every taxpayer's situation is different. It is also best practice to have your accountant run a midyear tax projection to determine whether you are on pace to have enough taxes withheld from your paychecks by year's end, based on your income. If it is determined that you are not on pace to withhold enough in taxes for the year, it may make sense to pay an estimated tax payment or increase tax withholding for the remainder of the year to avoid a big tax bill in April.

> If it is determined that you are not on pace to withhold enough in taxes for the year, it may make sense to pay an estimated tax payment

We discussed the tax treatment and complications of stock awards in the previous chapter. The main point to remember is that employers typically underwithhold tax when you exercise stock options or restricted stock vests, because the required withholding is often lower than your tax bracket for the year. Therefore, you need to plan carefully. If you do not plan for the potential underwithholding of taxes, then you may find yourself frustrated and scrambling to come up with the cash at tax filing time.

> If you do not plan for the potential underwithholding of taxes, then you may find yourself frustrated and scrambling to come up with the cash at tax filing time.

Tax-Saving Strategies

Maximum Fund Your 401(k) and Other Retirement Accounts

As discussed in chapter 2, making the maximum allowable 401(k) contribution should be at the top of your priority list for saving taxes and building a tax-deferred retirement nest egg. By doing this, you will not only take advantage of receiving a dollar-for-dollar tax deduction but also receive the full employer matching contribution, if available. The 401(k) limits increase over time, so ensure you are always maximum funding your 401(k) plan. At a minimum, double-check you are on track in June of each year, so you have plenty of time to adjust your deferral amount before year's end.

If your company offers a nonqualified deferred compensation plan, read chapter 3 to determine whether saving money into this plan makes sense, because it can greatly reduce your taxes.

Next, consider contributing to a traditional or Roth individual retirement account (IRA). As an executive, your income may be too high to be eligible to contribute directly to a Roth IRA, but if you do not already have a traditional IRA, you may be able to take advantage of annual Roth conversions. This is where you make an annual deposit into your IRA and immediately convert it to your Roth IRA. If you don't have any other IRAs on your balance sheet, this strategy can work nicely. If you do have other IRAs already, this strategy may not make sense due the pro-rata rules when it comes to converting to the Roth IRA. In 2021, anyone with enough earned income can contribute $6,000 to an IRA (or Roth IRA if you're eligible), and those aged fifty and above can deposit an extra $1,000. Funding a traditional IRA or Roth IRA won't save you tax today (in most cases), but it's another important part of being a disciplined saver for retirement. Many people are amazed how quickly they can build their IRA or Roth IRA account over time by what seems like a small deposit each year. And you don't pay tax in retirement on the after-tax deposits you make today to the IRA or Roth IRA.

Donor Advised Fund

If you are charitably inclined, you may want to consider donating appreciated stock—especially company stock—into a donor advised fund (DAF). A DAF is a special charitable account that enables you to prefund several years' worth of charitable gifts into a brokerage account and take the tax deduction in the year contributions are made to the fund, regardless of when dollars are ultimately sent to your favorite charities.

It is more tax advantageous to donate appreciated stock to a DAF rather than cash. If you have been receiving equity awards over the years, then you may own significant amounts of highly appreciated company stock. This low-basis company stock may be a perfect candidate for donating to a DAF. If you donate a security that has grown in value, a tax deduction can be taken for the full market value of the security as long as it was purchased more than a year ago. And because the securities are donated rather than sold, you won't have to pay capital gains taxes when the stock is liquidated inside the DAF.

If you are on a restricted trading list, the transfer of company stock to the DAF must take place during an open trading window.

Health Savings Accounts

If you are enrolled in a high-deductible health plan as defined by the IRS, you are eligible to contribute to a health savings account (HSA). Health savings accounts offer tax-deductible contributions, tax-deferred growth for investments inside the account, and tax-free distributions if used for qualified medical expenses. This is called the "triple tax play." A high-deductible health plan is generally a good option to consider if you are healthy and interested in using an HSA to save or invest money.

Because the account rolls over year after year and there is no "use it or lose it" rule with HSAs, participating in an HSA can be a tremendously valuable strategy. To take full advantage of the power of HSAs, it is recommended to pay your current medical expenses out of pocket during your working years rather than use funds from your HSA. That way, you can invest the funds in your HSA for as long as possible to take advantage of the tax-deferred growth and tax-free distributions for medical expenses in retirement. We encourage our clients to treat their HSA like a retirement savings account, not a daily spending account. Any funds leftover at death can be passed to a named beneficiary income tax–free.

In 2021, individuals can contribute $3,600 to their HSA if they are enrolled in a high-deductible medical plan. For family coverage, the limit is $7,200. Those aged fifty-five and older in 2021 can contribute an extra $1,000 on a before-tax basis. The HSA contribution limits increase over time. If your employer also contributes to your HSA, the amount you can personally contribute is reduced by the employer's contribution, to reach the aforementioned limits.

Transferrable Tax Credits

Some states offer tax credits for investment in film production, renewable energy projects, real estate projects such as low-income housing, and other initiatives to spur economic growth and expand job opportunities in the state. Some states allow the transfer of these tax credits from one taxpayer to another. Often the businesses that earn the credits are unable to use all their credits, so they sell their extra credits to individual taxpayers at a discount. The taxpayer can use the credits to reduce their state tax bill. These credits have been increasingly popular since 2018, when tax law changes limited the amount of state income tax a person can deduct on their federal tax return. This is a way to save money on state taxes outside of that deduction limitation.

These types of tax credit transfers can be done either directly from the company who earned the credits or indirectly through brokers. The process to purchase credits is relatively simple if you engage an experienced broker. Prices for tax credits vary, but they are typically sold for around eighty-five or ninety cents on the dollar. To better understand how this works, let's look at an example.

Assume you have a state tax liability of $80,000 in a given tax year. Without purchasing tax credits, this will cost you $80,000. However, if you buy $80,000 worth of tax credits for 90 cents on the dollar, this will cost you only $72,000 to pay your tax bill. Buying credits at a discount is treated as a capital gain, so you would have to pay capital gain taxes on the $8,000 discount you have received. Assuming a tax rate of 35 percent, you would pay $2,800 ($8,000 × 35%) in tax, which reduces your total savings from $8,000 to $5,200. If you buy the tax credits and hold them for one year before using them, then the $8,000 capital gain in this example would be taxed at the long-term capital gain tax rate.

One of the major drawbacks, however, is that you will need to have plenty of excess cash available to purchase the credits. Purchasing transferrable state tax credits is likely worthwhile only if your state tax liability is very high—say, $50,000 or more. As a W-2 employee, it's essentially double paying your state income taxes until you file your tax return and receive the refund from your state. However, if your employer allows you to stop having state income taxes withheld through payroll, this avoids "double paying" your state income taxes and having to wait for your tax refund to enjoy the benefits of buying these credits.

As a W-2 income earner, corporate executives have limited ways to save tax each year, but the strategies in this chapter should be considered and discussed with a tax specialist to ensure you are doing all you can to keep more of your annual earnings. We recommend hiring a good accountant who is familiar with executive compensation issues and strategies—it's worth paying for this expertise.

CHAPTER 6

Pensions

It's rare that companies offer a traditional pension plan anymore, but if yours does, read on!

Corporate executives who work for companies that still offer pensions are often faced with a choice when they retire or leave the company: choose a one-time lump sum payment or a monthly annuity that will provide a steady lifetime stream of income. The choice can be a real conundrum, and the pension decision is one of the most critical financial decisions a retiree must make.

> The pension decision is one of the most critical financial decisions a retiree must make.

In order to make this big decision, it is important for the executive to consider several factors: The health of their company's pension plan, the implied mathematical sweet spot of the various lump sum versus annuity options offered, and the inherent pros and cons of each payout option. In addition, the person's health status, family longevity, financial wherewithal of their partner, tax situation, and other cashflow streams in retirement all need to be considered.

Health of the Pension Plan

As we have discussed earlier, corporate executives can have a high concentration of their company's stock through outright stock holdings, equity awards, or their retirement plans. If executives retire and elect to receive their pension benefit as an annuity payment that will be funded by the company's pension plan, the reliance on the company's success remains. It also comes down to the degree the company's pension plan is funded.

As has been widely documented, rising life expectancies and historically low interest rates have put pressure on pension plans. This is the reason, in many cases, that pension plans are going the way of the dinosaur. There's been a trend of companies offering early buyouts of past employee's pension accounts or terminating the plan altogether by cashing out current retirees.

For executives whose companies are still offering pension plans, it is critical they look at the funding status of the plan before making their irrevocable decision. How close is the company to having the amount of assets in their pension plan to meet their projected obligations? What is the trajectory of the funded percentage? Is the plan getting healthier, or is the plan headed in the wrong direction? Most companies with a pension plan send out an update on the health of their pension plan at least once a year, but additional data may also be available in the company's notes to their audited financial statements. Retiring executives should take the time to investigate this because if the pension plan is not well funded or the plan's funding status is becoming more and more in question, electing a lump sum option may be a prudent decision.

> If the pension plan is not well funded or the plan's funding status is becoming more and more in question, electing a lump sum option may be a prudent decision.

The Math

In many cases the pension options offered to a retiree are actuarily equal. However, that doesn't mean that you shouldn't roll up your sleeves and pop the hood to understand the mathematical details behind the offerings.

For example, it may be worth calculating the present value of your annuity options by estimating your life expectancy and the life expectancy of your partner if there are survivor annuity options, as well as determining the internal rate of return. Compare the implied internal rate of return for the annuity options to a reasonable expected rate of return on a prudently diversified investment portfolio. Next, although it ignores inflation and rate of return, simply taking the lump sum and dividing it by a monthly annuity option can also be a quick and easy method to consider how many years an executive would have to live before the break-even point, where they would receive more dollars from an annuity than an initial lump sum. In some cases, there may be a clear mathematical winner, or you may be able to at least identify some perceived discrepancies between survivor annuity options that will help you make a more informed pension decision.

Another mathematical exercise that is often worth doing involves exploring the risk of inflation on your retirement scenario. Simply put, if you were to elect an annuity option, how much income would you receive in a year? What do you expect to receive from Social Security in a year? To those two figures, add a placeholder for a prudent annual withdrawal from your current liquid investment assets. (If you are thinking of electing a lump sum instead of an annuity, add the value of the lump sum to your current liquid investment assets.) What percentage of these figures is from your pension? What percentage of these figures is from Social Security? What percentage of these figures is from your nest egg? Pensions are rarely inflation protected, and Social Security benefits receive inconsistent cost of living increases, so when analyzing the underlying math behind your pension decision, be sure to consider how susceptible your financial situation could be to inflation and the slow erosion of your purchasing power.

> Pensions are rarely inflation protected, and Social Security benefits receive inconsistent cost of living increases, so when analyzing the underlying math behind your pension decision, be sure to consider how susceptible your financial situation could be to inflation and the slow erosion of your purchasing power.

Lump Sum versus Annuity—Pros and Cons

The choice of a one-time lump sum payment versus a steady stream of annuity income has pros and cons.

If you elect a one-time lump sum payment, a full "lifetime" benefit is immediately added to your personal balance sheet. If you are in poor health or family history tells you that you are likely to have a shorter than normal life expectancy, the lump sum may likely be the better choice. If you want to leave assets to your heirs, the lump sum may also be the better option. If you elect a one-time lump sum payment, roll it over to a traditional IRA so you don't create a huge tax bill. You can invest the funds in a diversified IRA portfolio that you control, potentially growing the funds and outpacing inflation. However, future investment returns are uncertain, so the pension benefit you've worked your whole career for will also fluctuate. If investment returns aren't what you hoped for, your pension benefit could lose value.

If you elect an annuity, you have the peace of mind of a stable and more predictable cash flow. There's less reliance on investment returns to supply retirement income, and if you or your partner live a long life, the total value of the pension benefits you receive could eventually exceed the value of the lump sum you were originally offered. However, if there is no guaranteed cost of living adjustment, a pension benefit won't be worth the same to you the first year of retirement as it is in the fifteenth year of retirement. This may mean you will need to dip more and more into your nest egg over time to maintain the desired standard of living. There is additional pressure on your investment strategy to perform well when a pension has no inflation protection. Also, if no survivor annuity options are available, or even with a survivor annuity option when you and your partner pass away, no financial benefit will be available for your heirs.

Other Considerations

There are a few other pension decision criteria we have observed through the years.

If survivor annuity options are offered, partners of executives tend to desire one of those options being elected if they are not financially astute. Losing a few hundred dollars each month by electing a survivor annuity option versus a single life annuity option on the life of the corporate executive can be a small price to pay for executives having the peace of mind that their partners would be in a better place financially if something happened to them. And the partners also have peace of mind that they would not have to simultaneously face the financial loss of their partner's entire pension while grieving the death of a loved one.

Next, some executives who have participated in stock option and deferred compensation programs find they have a multiyear cashflow stream available to them the first five to ten (or more) years in retirement from these two assets. In this case, taking a lump sum pension can make a lot of sense if you don't need the income for many years—you can invest and let it grow.

For example, you have accumulated $1 million in your deferred compensation plan and elected a ten-year payout at retirement. You also have not exercised your stock options early, they are worth $1 million as well, and they have five years left before they all expire. You are sixty years old when you retire. Your cashflow strategy looks like this.

- You will have $100,000 annually paid out of deferred compensation from age sixty to seventy.
- You realize $200,000 of income from age sixty to sixty-five from stock options.
- Required withdrawals from 401(k) and IRA accounts don't need to start until age seventy-two.
- Social Security can likely be delayed until age sixty-six or age seventy, letting the benefit grow even larger.
- You have a taxable brokerage account that can be used to supplement living expense needs during ages sixty to seventy-two.
- Given the above factors and your living expense needs, you may not need to start tapping your pension for at least the first five years of retirement.
- You take the lump sum, roll it to an IRA to avoid paying tax on the pension until you are ready to withdraw ... and then start withdrawing money several years down the road. (Required

distributions from IRAs must begin by age seventy-two so you don't defer the income forever.)

One of the pressures that makes the pension decision such a difficult one is that it is irrevocable (unless you elected to take an annuity and the company comes back to you with a lump sum buyout option or mandate). However, if you elect a lump sum, that is not entirely true. You could always elect a lump sum, directly roll it over to a traditional IRA, and then decide later that you wanted to buy an annuity through an insurance carrier with

> One of the pressures that makes the pension decision such a difficult one is that it is irrevocable

some or all the proceeds in the traditional IRA. Few people realize this, but it can take away some of the pressure of the pension decision if you know you always have a mulligan should you elect to take a one-time lump sum benefit only to later realize that wasn't the choice for you. However, beware that the do-over usually does not come without a cost, in the sense that it is very rare that an

> Few people realize this, but it can take away some of the pressure of the pension decision if you know you always have a mulligan

insurance carrier is able to offer as rich of an annuity benefit for the lump sum as your company originally offered.

When executives with pensions are making their election decision, it often comes down to whether they want a "three-legged retirement stool," where their retirement income will be coming in through their pension annuity, Social Security, and their investment portfolio, or a "two-legged stool," where their retirement income will be coming in through Social Security and their investment portfolio (including their pension lump sum). In our experience the best pension option is specific to each individual executive; there is not one right answer for everyone.

CHAPTER 7

Insurance Plans

Since the 1940s, US corporations have offered employer sponsored insurance as a competitive incentive and bargaining chip in the quest to attract and retain talent. Apart from your salary and bonus, your subsidized insurance coverage can be one of your most important elements of your compensation package. In this chapter, we will discuss the types of coverage available to you and provide guidance to ensure your biggest risks are properly insured.

Health Insurance

Of all the insurance policies you have, this may be the one that you interact with the most. Options, features, and costs of these plans vary wildly from carrier to carrier, and the options available to you are completely up to your employer. If you do have a choice in coverage, it is likely between some form of traditional plan and a high deductible plan.

	Traditional Plan	High Deductible Plan
Monthly Premiums	Higher	Lower
Deductibles	Lower	Higher
Out-of-Pocket Costs	Lower	Higher
Medical Savings Account(s)	Lower pre-tax limits (FSA)	Higher pre-tax limits (HSA)
HSA Eligible	No	Yes

Traditional medical insurance plans typically make sense for those who have regular ongoing medical expenses, or a major surgery planned where there will be known high medical bills. Although premiums are higher, there is less out-of-pocket risk. You often have the option of setting aside a limited amount of dollars into a pre-tax flexible spending account (FSA) that's a use-it-or-lose-it account to pay for current year medical expenses. The FSA limit in 2021 is $2,750, and this limit increases over time.

High deductible plans shift some of the risk from the insurer back to the policyholder (you). In exchange for taking on more risk and financial liability in the form of a higher deductible, you will pay less on premiums. If you and your family don't need much medical care throughout the year, you may come out ahead by hundreds or thousands of dollars by electing the high deductible plan. However, you should always be prepared to meet the full deductible and be aware of the out-of-pocket maximum for covered family members.

As discussed in chapter 5, one great advantage of the high deductible plan is that you have access to a health savings account (HSA) to which you can contribute before-tax dollars to pay for your future medical costs. Not only will these contributions come out of your income before tax, but you can invest these dollars, the growth will be tax deferred, and withdrawals are tax-free if you use them for qualified medical expenses. Currently the HSA is your only "triple tax play" savings account!

> Currently the HSA is your only "triple tax play" savings account!

Your decision of which medical plan to choose is a highly personal decision based on your own health, preexisting conditions, and medications for both you and your family. Your human resources department should be able to provide you with the information you need to fully understand your options and make an informed decision during open enrollment.

Life Insurance

Over the course of your career, life insurance will play an important role, especially if you have a family or others dependent upon your income.

Young professionals with children and a mortgage need life insurance to provide for their families in the event of a premature death. Replacing your income during your working career may be the single largest factor in the calculation of how much life insurance to buy. For example, if you are earning $200,000 annually and plan to work another ten years, that equates to $2 million of potential lost income if you were to pass away prematurely. Mature professionals and retirees may no longer need life insurance for income replacement needs, yet they may choose to keep the coverage for other reasons such as estate liquidity, inheritance equalization, or planned giving to charities. Regardless of your age and stage in life, there are several concepts to understand about life insurance.

Group Life Insurance—The Base

Most employers offer a nominal amount of life insurance equal to one or two times an employee's base pay. This is usually a free benefit to the employee and can be a good foundation for life insurance planning, but for most executives, this will not be nearly enough to cover all their life insurance needs. Your employer may provide a small amount for your partner as well.

How Much Do You Need?

Depending on your family dynamics and needs, this number can vary greatly, but there are generally three expenses most people look to life insurance to cover: outstanding debts (including mortgage), education costs for children, and ongoing income for surviving family members.

> There are generally three expenses most people look to life insurance to cover: outstanding debts (including mortgage), education costs for children, and ongoing income for surviving family members.

There are several professionals and calculation tools that can help you determine how much life insurance you need, but a good rule of thumb is to maintain ten times your earnings. Don't rely solely on this benchmark to make sure your loved ones are provided for in the event you end up truly needing your life insurance. A comprehensive financial plan can pinpoint how much insurance you need based on your goals, assets, and specific family situation.

How to Supplement

You may need more life insurance than your employer provides, so the decision point is how to acquire this additional coverage. Many companies will allow employees to purchase additional life insurance with little or no medical underwriting. Supplemental life insurance can be advantageous for people who have health concerns that otherwise may prohibit them from acquiring affordable private insurance. There are three concerns with buying supplemental group coverage. The first is that if you are healthy, you could pay less for your premiums by getting a private policy through a life insurance company. Second, these group policies may have limited portability if you lose or change your job. Make sure you can take this coverage with you if you leave, if that's important to you. Finally, the group premiums tend to increase every few years based on age brackets.

What Type Should You Get?

There are several types of life insurance policies available, and for the average consumer, the options can be confusing. Here are the basics of the main types of policies and how you would generally use them.

Term—Term life insurance covers a temporary need for a period of time, or a term. These policies are often sold in blocks of time such as ten or twenty years, or they may be sold with coverage lasting "to age sixty-five." Term insurance is typically very affordable. For most people, term insurance is adequate and appropriate because you need the most life insurance during the years you are building your balance sheet. Once you achieve financial independence, the need for life insurance should be minimal or nonexistent. However, when you are deciding the length of the term you want to purchase, it's often best for the term to end after your planned future retirement date in case you don't hit your retirement date goal, or your goals change.

Term life insurance offers maximum protection for minimal premium outlay. What you pay in premiums is fixed for a period of time, often lasting for the entire term of the policy. However, after the term ends, the premiums tend to skyrocket because those who keep the policy going are typically the unhealthy population.

Permanent—There are a variety of policies that offer some form of "permanent" death benefit and accumulate cash value. These policies range from more conservative, traditional whole life policies to more speculative variable life policies. There are varying opinions in the financial world as to when permanent life insurance is a viable strategy. The premiums are much higher than term insurance, but if you do need life insurance for many decades, this can be a better solution. The cash value feature can look attractive, but there are costs associated with the permanent policies that aren't included with term life policies, so buyer beware.

If you have long-term death benefit needs for estate planning purposes, a comprehensive financial plan can help identify the right type of life insurance policy. It's best to get a few opinions before you commit to buying a permanent policy to ensure you're not being sold something you don't need.

Disability Insurance

Many people brush off disability insurance because they cannot fathom a scenario where they become "disabled". In fact, during working years more than 1-in-4 workers will experience some type of disability[1]. Aside from the likelihood, consider the enormous financial loss if you could no longer earn a living. It is critical the correct amount of disability insurance be in

> It is critical the correct amount of disability insurance be in place to afford a family a continued standard of living in the event of an illness or injury.

place to afford a family a continued standard of living in the event of an illness or injury.

Most standard employer plans cover 60 percent of the employee's base salary. There are several points to be aware of. First, the 60 percent coverage amount is an average, not a standard; check your employer's plan to confirm your amount. Second, this applies only to base earnings in most plans; bonuses, commissions, and incentive pay are generally excluded from disability insurance benefit calculations. Finally, there is often a cap on monthly benefits, such as a $10,000 monthly maximum.

For example, let's say your base salary is $250,000 and you earned an additional $100,000 in bonus and incentives. If your plan's coverage is only based on your salary and has a $10,000 monthly cap, your benefit is 48 percent of your salary yet covers only 34 percent of your total earnings. If you don't think you could cut back to 34 percent of your pre-disability earnings, you need to consider supplemental coverage.

Supplemental Disability Insurance

You can typically supplement basic group disability coverage through your employer or by purchasing private insurance. When you are building your balance sheet, it is good to buy as much supplemental protection as an insurance company will underwrite (generally up to 80 percent of total earnings). Be aware of elimination periods (aka waiting periods), which are often 90 or 180 days, and make sure you have sufficient emergency funds to bridge that gap. Also, most disability insurance policy coverage stops at age sixty-five, so if you work past age sixty-five and then become disabled, your disability policy may not pay a benefit. If you retire before age sixty-five and don't plan to go back to work, this argues for discontinuing your policy.

Taxes

Unlike life insurance, under current law, disability insurance benefits may be subject to income tax. Look at your paystub to see whether you are paying premiums for your group disability or if your employer covers those premiums. If you go on claim and your employer has been paying the premiums, you will have to report the benefit received as taxable income and pay the IRS based on your tax bracket, further eroding the coverage percentage. If you are paying your premiums with pre-tax dollars, you will also have to report the benefit received as taxable income if you go on claim. The ideal scenario is to pay your disability premiums with after-tax dollars, meaning your employer is not running them as a pre-tax item through payroll.

Long-Term Care Insurance

One insurance need that busy professionals tend to push off thinking about until retirement is long-term care insurance. However, given changes in the long-term care insurance industry and increasing life expectancies, executives need to start thinking about this coverage in their forties and fifties.

> This rising long-term care insurance cost trend is likely to continue, so planning for long-term care needs should be done sooner rather than later.

Most people have experienced the need for long-term health care with a family or friend and have seen how crippling the costs can be if not adequately prepared for. Care can be received in the home, assisted living facility, or adult daycare, and it can go all the way up to twenty-four-hour nursing home facilities. Medicare will not offset the costs of chronic care in retirement and qualifying for Medicaid may be challenging for more affluent families. For the past several decades, acquiring private long-term care insurance has been a great precautionary approach. However, in an attempt to gain market share quickly, many long-term care insurance providers did not adequately price their premiums, and this has led to rate increases and the exit of multiple insurers from the long-term care market.

There are several options still available today, but the traditional long-term care policies are more limited and costly than options from even a decade ago. An increasingly popular product that is more widely available today is known as a hybrid policy. This is a life insurance policy with a long-term care rider. The concept is you are spending down your death benefit during life if you incur long-term care expenses, but if you don't incur those expenses during life, a death benefit (or portion of it) pays to your heirs. Many people seem to like this structure because they know they're getting a benefit out of the insurance policy regardless of what the future holds for their long-term care needs. In addition, some products allow you to pay for them with a one-time premium, or over ten or twenty years, versus requiring a lifetime premium payment.

Most companies do not offer long-term care insurance as an employee benefit, so you'll likely need to look to an individual insurance company for this coverage. This rising long-term care insurance cost trend is likely to continue, so planning for long-term care needs should be done sooner rather than later.

Property and Casualty Insurance

Another type of insurance to address is your property and casualty coverage. It is extremely important to make sure that your real assets such as your home, autos, and any recreation vehicles or vacation properties are properly insured. You should work with an independent broker to help you explore coverage options and understand what your policies cover. Not all insurance policies work the same; what is covered varies by company, and the low-cost providers often have gaps in what they'll pay for. You don't want to learn this after filing a claim.

We encourage our clients to secure umbrella or excess liability coverage equal to their total net worth. This coverage overlays the underlying liability limits in your home and auto coverage (like an umbrella) to help ensure that once the liability limits of those policies are met, your personal assets do not become exposed in the event of an accident or lawsuit. We live in a litigious society, and accidents can happen at any moment. If you have a high-profile job, work for a high-profile company, drive an expensive car, live in an upscale home, own watercraft or recreational vehicles, or have teenage drivers, your exposure to liability risk is high. In addition, if you serve on a charitable board or for-profit board, make sure they provide directors and officers insurance to protect you personally against any claims arising against the charity or company you are serving.

> If you have a high-profile job, work for a high-profile company, drive an expensive car, live in an upscale home, own watercraft or recreational vehicles, or have teenage drivers, your exposure to liability risk is high.

Review your coverage regularly with your agent, shop around for comparable coverage and quotes every few years, and increase your umbrella coverage as your net worth continues to grow.

Client Story

A few years ago, one of our advisors got a call from a client who was an executive at a large food company. Late on a Friday night, this client left a voice mail for her advisor that said, "I can't thank you enough for telling us to get a $3 million umbrella policy in place. My husband was just in a car accident, four cars of people were injured, and it was his fault. But because of this umbrella coverage, we are sleeping well at night knowing our personal assets are protected."

Chapter Endnote

1   Social Security Administration. "Disability Fact Sheet". 2020. www.ssa.gov/disabilityfacts/facts.html.

CHAPTER 8

Estate Planning

As an executive, you can appreciate the importance of planning for the inevitable curveballs thrown at your business. Even the best laid plans are challenged at some point by forces outside of your control. Proper planning can make all the difference between weathering the storm or not. So too is the case with your estate plan.

The death, disability, or illness of you and your family is less than pleasant to contemplate, but these are realities of life and can easily derail an otherwise solid financial plan. Therefore, it is critical that you invest in a quality estate plan. View your estate plan as set in sand, not stone, and it will need to be updated over time as your family situation changes, your financial position evolves, tax laws change, or an unexpected life event occurs.

There are very few clients who come through our doors for the first time and have their estate plan buttoned up. It's often one of the top action items we help them address as we put their financial strategy in place.

A good estate plan will have, at a minimum, three components.

A good estate plan will have, at a minimum, three components.

1. Will—Directs where some of your assets are to be distributed upon after death. (But note that a will does not direct where all

    your assets go!) In addition, some people establish revocable living trusts.

2.   Durable Power of Attorney for Finances—Allows a trusted individual to make business and financial decisions if you are incapacitated but still living.

3.   Healthcare Directive/Power of Attorney for Healthcare and Living Will—Allows you to state your wishes for medical care when you are unable to do so. In addition, you can appoint a trusted individual to make important medical decisions when you are incapacitated.

Will

A will is a legal document that allows you to state your wishes regarding how your property will be distributed after your death, who is in control of settling your estate, and (if applicable) who will be the guardian of your minor children.

Your will appoints people to important roles. First, your will should appoint an executor who will be charged with carrying out the terms of your will and managing the business of your estate by paying creditors, filing tax returns, and distributing assets to beneficiaries. Although this role is usually temporary in nature, some estates can take years to settle, and even "small" estates can involve quite a bit of work. Executors should have good business sense and be comfortable with managing an administratively intense process. They should know who your professional advisors are because those advisors can make executors' jobs easier. The more your estate plan and overall financial affairs are buttoned up before death, the easier your executor's job will be.

Another important appointment made in a will for people with minor children is that of a guardian. This will be the person(s) legally responsible for your children's physical care, health, and welfare. Note this person does not need to be responsible for managing the assets you leave to your child. Rather, focus on someone who shares your same family values and can do the best job of raising your children. Also, discuss the role of guardian with the person of your choosing before formalizing it in your will. Be sure that the person you have chosen is willing and able to fulfill this job if needed.

Other important decisions to make when creating or updating your will include whether you want to be buried or cremated, and how you would like your debts and expenses associated with your estate paid.

> Discuss the role of guardian with the person of your choosing before formalizing it in your will.

For many people, simply leaving all remaining property to a surviving spouse or partner in their will is an appropriate strategy. In other cases, more sophisticated planning is needed to direct that certain assets be passed to different people or trusts. A will should distribute your assets to the people and places, and in the proper amounts, that you desire.

Trusts

A trust is a formal arrangement in which a third party, called a trustee, holds assets on behalf of a beneficiary or beneficiaries. A trust may be created in a separate document or embedded in your will. The trust may come into play as soon as you sign the document or not until after you've passed away.

A living trust is established during your lifetime, and you retitle assets into the trust during life. The trustee of the trust becomes the owner of those assets; typically, you serve as your own trustee of your lifetime trust. During life, your living trust is revocable, meaning you can change it at any time and for any reason. A separate tax return does not need to be filed for a revocable living trust. One benefit of a lifetime living trust is the person serving as your backup (successor) trustee can quickly jump into place should you be incapacitated and unable to handle your financial affairs. It can be easier to transact on assets already titled in a living trust for the successor trustee, rather than using a financial power of attorney document (more on this below).

Many wills are designed for assets to be left to a trust upon the death of the owner of those assets. In some cases this is done to avoid estate tax and probate costs, or to maximize the ability of one's assets to be shielded from taxes down the road. However, a trust is a powerful tool that can be used for many other purposes aside from tax avoidance. Some nontax situations in which trusts can be effectively used include holding an inheritance for an adult child who has proven irresponsible with managing money, or asset protection when money could be otherwise in jeopardy due to potential litigation, divorce, or business failure. Consider your family circumstances and who will inherit assets from you. Do any beneficiaries have unique situations, characteristics, or risks that might warrant using a trust for their inheritance? Is your estate sizeable to the point it could ruin your children or derail their value system if they received their inheritance all at once? Do your children or ultimate beneficiaries of your estate work in a litigious industry such as health care? Trusts can be tremendous tools to help preserve wealth for future generations.

Important Note about Beneficiary Designations

A will does not direct the disposition of all types of assets. In fact, there are many of these non-probate assets whose disposition is governed by a beneficiary designation instead of a will. Such assets can include the following.

- Retirement accounts like 401(k)s, 403(b)s, IRAs, Roth IRAs, deferred compensation accounts, and pensions
- Health savings accounts (HSAs)
- Life insurance and annuity contracts
- Bank or brokerage accounts with a "transfer on death" (TOD) or "payable on death" (POD) designation
- Stock options (if your company plan allows)

Assets owned jointly with someone else as joint tenants or tenants by the entirety will not pass according to your will. They pass automatically to the named joint owner.

In the case of corporate executives, it is common to see substantial assets or even the majority of net worth reside in these non-probate assets. A lot of time and money can be spent crafting a solid will or trust, but those documents may not actually dictate where a majority of someone's assets may go at death.

> A lot of time and money can be spent crafting a solid will or trust, but those documents may not actually dictate where a majority of someone's assets may go at death.

Consequently, it is extremely important that you put beneficiary designations in place when opening a retirement account or buying life insurance for example. It is equally important to revisit these designations every few years. We have seen hundreds of thousands of dollars fall into unintended hands and leave loved ones empty-handed because of failure to update beneficiaries. Common situations that are cause for updates are after a divorce or birth or a child. If your company changes plan administrators for the company's retirement accounts, that's another time to ensure your beneficiary designation is up to date at the plan administrator. We've seen many instances where prior beneficiary designations on file disappear because data is not transferred to the new retirement plan's administration company. Despite the wishes stated in your will, understand that some of your assets will be distributed according to the beneficiary designation form, so don't overlook this important aspect of estate planning.

Durable Power of Attorney for Finances

The second component of your estate plan is a durable power of attorney (DPOA). This allows a trusted party to make financial decisions and act on your behalf in the event you are incapacitated or unavailable during life and cannot make informed decisions or communicate them yourself. (You don't have to be incapacitated for a durable power of attorney to be effective; you can elect otherwise when setting up the document.) As with other appointments in your estate plan, have a discussion with the person you intend to appoint to ensure he or she is willing to serve in this capacity. A person can serve as a DPOA for an extended period and ultimately become unwilling or choose to hand over duties to someone else. Therefore, in addition to selecting a primary agent, it is highly recommended that you choose a backup agent or two.

A best practice is to provide a copy of your DPOA to financial institutions you do business with such as banks and investment brokerages for their review and acceptance. Preferably, this should be done before executing a final copy in case any changes are required. Some institutions have historically been reluctant to accept DPOAs because they lack specific language or have been deemed to be too old. Efforts are being made in many states to reduce the circumstances in which DPOAs can be rejected, but this remains a widespread problem.

Healthcare Directive and Living Will

The third component of your estate plan are documents that allow you to appoint a trusted individual or individuals to make decisions and communicate on your behalf regarding healthcare options. You'll state your wishes for healthcare treatments such as life support if you are unable to communicate them yourself. Headlines have been filled in recent history with tragic examples of family infighting about who should make life support decisions for a loved one during what is already an emotionally difficult time. Executing these important documents in advance removes any doubt about your desire for healthcare treatment and who is charged with communicating those wishes.

Other Considerations

Parents of older teens or children in college: Your adult children need estate planning documents as well. If your children are over the age of eighteen, they are legally an adult. Although you may intuitively think that, as their parent, you can make financial and healthcare decisions or act on their behalf, the law sees it differently. When your children become legal adults, they will need a DPOA and healthcare POA in order for you to step in for them, so be sure they have these documents as well.

Next, where to store your documents is an important consideration as well. Estate documents are often kept in secure locations such as safe deposit boxes at a bank. Although this may work adequately for a will, provided you have given someone else access to your safe deposit box if needed, it is not prudent for powers of attorney. They are often needed in emergency situations when emotions are high, so the last thing you want to be dealing with is a problem accessing these documents (think trying to access the bank branch on a Sunday afternoon). Instead, store the power of attorney documents in a secure but accessible location such as a fireproof safe at your home. These safes can be purchased at many retailers for minimal cost. Your agents should be aware of the code or where to find the code.

As you contemplate the important decisions to be made when creating an estate plan, be mindful that life happens, and circumstances will change. Few if any of the decisions you make are permanent. We tell most clients that their current estate plan likely has a shelf life of about five years. After that time, changes in family or financial circumstances, or changes in tax law, will probably require an update or revision to the current plan. Accept this as a cost of doing business and a gift to your loved ones. And please, don't even consider using a computer software package or online will preparation service. There are so many issues and holes with those programs—that's called being penny wise and pound foolish. It's much less expensive to pay a lawyer now to update your estate plan than have your family pay lawyers, accountants, and the IRS to clean up your mess if you fail to plan.

> It's much less expensive to pay a lawyer now to update your estate plan than have your family pay lawyers, accountants, and the IRS to clean up your mess if you fail to plan.

CHAPTER 9

Climbing the Corporate Ladder and Avoiding Burnout

It's so important for executives to understand all the compensation programs available to them, and which ones to take advantage of, as they grow in their careers. "I wish I had done this years ago" should not be a phrase that comes out of your mouth after reading this book, yet it's a common phrase we've heard with new executive clients over the years. The earlier in your career you can get a jump on your finances, the more successful you'll likely be.

Another best practice for rising executives is to find a mentor within the organization who will help shepherd their career moves. Mentors can hopefully share advice about money moves they've made that have been fruitful. They may also share mistakes they've made that can be equally valuable to learn.

As you grow in your career, not only will your corporate responsibilities increase, but so will the complexity of your compensation package and financial planning. Some of the big items include the following:

1. Stock grants. As you climb the ladder, you may start receiving stock awards, different types of stock awards, and larger awards. Read chapter 4 about stock options and restricted stock to refresh your planning strategy.

2. Taxes. Do you have more income coming in than ever before? Your tax bill is going to climb too. Read chapter 5 again and consult with an accountant who specializes in executive compensation tax issues. As a result of promotions, big bonuses, and stock plans paying out, executives can move in and out of high tax brackets over their working years. Partnering with a competent tax advisor can help smooth out and minimize taxes, allowing you to further maximize your wealth.

3. Insurance. Now that you are worth more in corporate America, is it time to increase your life, disability, and liability coverage? See chapter 7.

4. Savings strategy. When you first start working, saving may have been a foreign concept because you were just trying to make ends meet. When you get to the point where you have more cash coming in than needs to go out, start a regular monthly savings strategy right away. This will help you build considerable wealth over time in a pain-free way. If you don't need the extra cash to live on, you won't miss it when it's transferred from checking to savings or investment accounts.

5. Above all, resist "lifestyle creep." With each new raise, avoid the temptation to spend this new money. Don't run out and buy a bigger house or a new shiny expensive car. Don't start flying first class on vacations. Lifestyle creep is a major reason that people don't accumulate more financial gains from their promotions. Instead, look to increase the amount you save each month and do that first; spend the leftover money from the raise second.

The key to financial success is spending less than you earn and investing the difference wisely over a long period. Remember that as your lifestyle increases during your working years, it's common that your post-corporate lifestyle does too—thus the need for ongoing planning and increasing your savings rate as you climb the ladder at work.

> The key to financial success is spending less than you earn and investing the difference wisely over a long period.

63

Avoiding Burnout

As you take on bigger and more demanding roles, remember there is more to life than your job title, your compensation plan, or the amount of money in your bank account. The more you can balance your daily priorities, including taking care of yourself, the longer you can last in corporate America on what we call running on the hamster wheel.

Health

With all the demands of a fast-paced career and the duties outside of work that are a reality of life, many people struggle to prioritize their health, whether that be enough sleep, exercise, or proper nutrition. Fidelity Investment's 2019 Millionaire Outlook study found health concerns top the list for all investors, including millionaires.[1] You may want to consider retiring as soon as you can to focus on self-care and improving your quality of your life. We witness many clients losing weight, shedding anxiety, and reporting a general increase in joy in their first year of retirement.

Family

Work-life balance is one of those lofty goals that can seem to always be out of reach. Especially as you are trying to climb the ladder at work, this will mean sacrificing time at home. If you let this get out of control, it can lead to damaged relationships, divorce, lifelong distancing from your children, and time you can't get back. Some of our clients who run hard and fast on the hamster wheel for too long choose to step away from their corporate careers as soon as they can, with the goal of spending more time with family. If you do a good job of saving, most people find it's wonderful to retire at an early enough age to still have health and time to travel and enjoy life. Many of our clients want to seize that time and enjoy it with loved ones, tipping the scales of balance back in their favor. Be aware of how much you are tipping your scales as you're climbing the ladder.

Client Story

One of our clients was a very successful corporate executive, a top female in her Fortune 100 company. Unfortunately, a health scare stopped her in her tracks one day, but after a few years of treatments, she was back running at a fast pace. Although she was worth millions of dollars, she never took the time to have a financial plan done or run the numbers to know how much longer she needed to work. Based on a referral from a colleague, she hired us, and we did the calculations. When we told her she had enough money in the bank right now to stop working, she sat back in her chair, leaned over, put her hands over her face, and started to cry. She had no idea she was in as good of financial shape as she was, and she realized she'd given so much of her life to working due to fear she didn't have enough. She retired about two years after receiving this news, primarily to make sure she transitioned her work responsibilities well, and she has never looked back. She knows her years in retirement are limited due to health issues, but at least she can decide how she spends those years.

Your Plans Change

Your team goes through a reorganization, and you don't get along with the new leader. The demands of work become more than you want to manage at this phase of life. A family member becomes sick. You become sick. Your partner gets a great job out of state, and you have to relocate. Regardless of the curveballs life throws your way, change is inevitable, and you have to be nimble to shift your career plans. These unexpected occurrences can be unsettling, particularly for someone who has been deliberate in navigating one's career to advance to the next level. The ability to control one's future has shifted.

Given life's changes, we've seen clients choose to leave their corporate career and consult for a few years. Some do this to bridge their income gap; others do it to stay mentally sharp and connected to their peers and industry while having more time at home. Others simply want to try something new, scratch their entrepreneurial itch, and be their own boss. Regardless, having enough savings in the bank is critical during these times of change, especially if you have to take the off ramp temporarily from an otherwise strategic career plan.

Chapter Endnote

1   Fidelity. "The Intersection of Advice and Well Being". Millionaire Outlook 2019. https://clearingcustody.fidelity.com/app/item/RD_9889533.html

CHAPTER 10

Receiving a Severance Package

Another one of life's curveballs is learning your company is planning a round of layoffs. Emotions such as fear, anger, concern, caution, and confusion typically follow. However, when companies are going to be trimming their workforce, they sometimes offer additional perks and dangle carrots to the impacted employees in exchange for those employees signing a release, to avoid potential future lawsuits. Few of the corporate executives we have worked with have been pleased to be involuntarily severed, and understandably so. But with so much of your long-term financial plan abruptly changing, the sooner you can get to calmly, correctly, and thoroughly answering the many questions racing through your mind, the better off you will be.

> With so much of your long-term financial plan abruptly changing, the sooner you can get to calmly, correctly, and thoroughly answering the many questions racing through your mind, the better off you will be.

Some of the most common questions we hear from executives who have learned they will be receiving a severance package include the following.

- Do I need to get another job?
- What happens to my equity awards?
- How can I minimize my taxes?

If you involuntarily receive a severance package, you are likely leaving your role and your company earlier than you had planned. There are fewer years of predictable income, bonuses, and equity awards to fund your lifestyle and build your retirement nest egg. If you have a pension, it will be less robust than you were anticipating because your expected years of service is being cut short. However, additional or accelerated compensation is often part of a severance package, and those funds can be a nice boost to your financial independence trajectory while providing an opportunity to check other financial boxes (e.g., setting aside funds to provide for your children's college or paying off your mortgage).

Whether you need to get another job or not can be influenced by many things. Is there a high probability that your desired lifestyle in retirement can be sustained by your current assets and retirement income streams? What happens to your health insurance and other benefits? If you aren't yet eligible for Medicare, can you get the type of health insurance you and your family need in the marketplace? Are you ready to be fully retired, or do you have more in the tank? Are you going to be able to live with the reality that the final chapter of your professional life ended with a severance package, or do you genuinely need to write a different ending to find peace? As you can see, there are not only financial implications to deciding whether to get another job, there are numerous emotional implications.

Here are some of the financial considerations.

What Happens to Your Equity Awards?

One of the areas in which we have seen corporate executives most impacted by involuntary severance packages is their equity awards. When executives are severed, there are usually special provisions that govern the amount of awards to be received and the time frame in which those awards will be received. It can be quite different from normal plan rules. Upon learning that you are going to be severed, getting clarity around the severance provisions related to your equity awards and

> Upon learning that you are going to be severed, getting clarity around the severance provisions related to your equity awards and quickly crafting a new optimal plan for your financial situation should be two of your biggest priorities.

quickly crafting a new optimal plan for your financial situation should be two of your biggest priorities.

In the case of stock options and restricted shares, how many of your grants are you going to be able to keep? This potential loss of expected future value can play a huge role in your retirement capacity and whether you will need to find another job.

If the expiration dates of your stock options are impacted by severance, it's important to have a well-thought-out strategy, especially to minimize taxes. If there will be a shorter time frame to exercise some or all your options, consider the best way to hedge potential movements in the company's stock price. Perhaps you can spread the exercise of your stock options over multiple tax years or defer exercising your remaining options until the year following your additional severance compensation, so that you aren't recognizing a lot of income in the highest tax brackets. Exercising stock options in waves can provide comfort against making a one-way bet on the company stock price as well; perhaps this is a quarterly strategy. If you believe your company's stock price or the greater market is at a high point, you may opt for immediately taking the value off the table. There are numerical strategies and optimal "you" strategies, and successfully navigating the two is very important to this potentially large asset on your balance sheet.

> There are numerical strategies and optimal "you" strategies, and successfully navigating the two is very important to this potentially large asset on your balance sheet.

How Can You Minimize Your Taxes?

There are strategies to minimize taxes, and at severance time, this needs to be looked at carefully. Projecting the dollar amount of regular income streams plus new forced payouts can go a long way in managing cash flow and taxes.

If the tax year you are going to be severed in is inevitably going to be an unusually large income year, if you are charitably inclined, it can also be a strategic time to do some major gifting. Financially, you are never better off giving money away, but tax wise, if you are going to give money to charity anyway, you should do so in a manner to get the biggest tax gain. Making major gifts can be a good idea in a big tax year, and many of the executives we have worked with also turn to donor advised funds; for more on donor advised funds, see chapter 5.

For example, if you typically give $20,000 a year to charity, consider giving $60,000 to a donor advised fund in the year you are severed, especially if you will be in the highest tax bracket. Then, you may choose to distribute $20,000 of the $60,000 gift in the current year. The remaining $40,000 is essentially "prefunding" the next two years' worth of giving. The charitable causes you are passionate about and wish to support can still receive their "annual gifts," but by making a larger donation in a higher tax year, you are being more strategic with tax savings.

In addition, be sure to maximum fund your 401(k) plan the year you are (or may be) severed. Typically, employers give more than a month's notice about job eliminations, so increase your 401(k) contribution percentage as soon as you hear the potential rumblings about downsizing.

If you've participated in a deferred compensation plan, check the plan's rules because you may find that the entire balance will be paid shortly after you leave the company. If so, it's all subject to tax at that point.

An involuntary severance package often means you need to quickly develop a plan to successfully transition from the company. The severance package itself can mean additional income and the accelerated and forced payouts of deferred compensation plans, supplemental retirement plans, stock options, restricted stock, and even pensions. These were long-term assets you have earned and worked hard for; they just happen to be paying out sooner and faster than originally anticipated. Even though the shock may be real and the emotions may be intense, you must get the transition from your company right. If you plan well for your transition and your severance payments, you may find it accelerates your ability to meet your financial goals, rather than being a setback.

> Even though the shock may be real and the emotions may be intense, you must get the transition from your company right.

CHAPTER 11

Working in the Gig Economy versus Corporate America

We see many corporate executive clients jump off the hamster wheel and consult or start their own small company and work for themselves versus working for someone else. Perhaps it happens when you least expect it, such as a downsizing at your company, a change of heart in your career path, interesting work you can't find at your current employer, or a passion to do something entrepreneurial. There is a growing trend toward workers in the gig economy, with many coming out of the traditional corporate America career path.

According to a 2019 study by Deloitte called "The Alternative Workforce: It's Now Mainstream," the number of workers who are self-employed was expected to grow to 42 million by 2020.[1] This includes contractors, freelancers, gig workers (paid to do a task) and the crowd (outsourced networks). According to the corporate responders in their survey, 33 percent reported extensively using alternative workers for IT, 25 percent for operations, and 15 percent for research and development.

Another report by Forbes in 2019 reported workers in the gig economy were expected to make up 40 percent of the workforce by 2020.[2]

The gig economy is here to stay, and you very well could be part of it in the next decade. Regardless of how you find yourself self-employed, there are several financial factors you need to have a basic understanding of, given the high probability the gig economy will find you at some point during your career.

	Corporate America	**Gig Economy**
Salary	Yes	No
Paid by Hour/Project	No	Yes
Company Provided Insurance	Yes	No
Paid Vacation Time	Yes	No
Bonuses	Yes	No
401k Match	Yes	No
Pension	Maybe	No
Taxes	High; W-2	More tax write-offs
Section 199a Deduction	No	Possible 20% deduction of business income
Qualified Retirement Plan Options	Limited—lower funding limits	Wide variety—higher funding limits
Work Schedule	They decide	You decide
Lifestyle	They control	You control

Working for yourself can be harder than working for someone else. You need to market yourself and create your own brand, whereas while working in corporate America, you don't have the need or pressure to establish a personal brand. Sure, you network within the office due to corporate politics or getting that next promotion, but nobody cares how many followers you have on LinkedIn, or how many times a week you tweet about your company or the projects you are progressing on. Yet when you are self-employed, you not only need to sell yourself, but you also need to establish and manage a lot of other personal financial aspects that a corporation was providing to you.

There's plenty of good news for those working in the gig economy as it relates to their finances. You can establish your own retirement plan and have many options such as a Solo 401(k), a SEP IRA, or a defined benefit pension plan. In many cases you can save more money on a before-tax basis into these retirement accounts than you can in a company provided 401(k) plan. Saving more for your retirement and saving more in tax now are both good benefits.

Next, there are health, life, and disability insurance plans available for those self-employed, and you can take a tax deduction for the premiums you pay on certain types of insurance, primarily medical and dental insurance, just like in corporate America. The premiums are likely higher than if you worked at a Fortune 500 company that employs thousands of workers, but you also may have more choices than the one health insurance carrier your employer selected for the year. One reason to have personal life and disability insurance outside of an employer is that if you find yourself leaving corporate America, either you can't take your life and disability policies with you, or if you can, they are extremely expensive to maintain. Term life insurance is usually a good choice to have as a personally owned policy; it's not tied to where you work, the premiums are lower, and it stays fixed for the term of the policy (e.g., twenty years). Whereas in corporate America, insurance rates are age-banded so the older you get, the more you pay.

Finally, taxes, taxes, taxes. As a self-employed individual, you pay the "employer" share of the Social Security and Medicare tax; it's double what you are paying as an employee in corporate America. This amounts to an extra 7.65 percent annual tax. (For 2021, the 6.2 percent tax portion is based only on the first $142,800 that one earns; the 1.45 percent is on all wage income.) However, there are many expenses you may be able to deduct against your self-employed income that you can't as a W-2 employee in corporate America. Don't take this list as specific tax advice; these are just some examples of deductible expenses.

> However, there are many expenses you may be able to deduct against your self-employed income that you can't as a W-2 employee in corporate America.

- Cell phone
- Computers, laptops, paper for home printer

- Home office
- Briefcase
- Dinner with friends or colleagues if you talk about legitimate business topics
- Travel expenses if you are working while away from home
- Car lease payments and related car expenses

If you are self-employed, it's important to hire a good accountant. This area of the tax law is tricky and not as straightforward as having all your pay on one W-2 tax form.

Lifestyle must be considered as well. It's not just about the money! When you are self-employed, you could find yourself working more hours, working harder, and having different stress due to not knowing where your next paycheck will come from. It also gives you a lot more control over your life and time because you are operating on your schedule, not someone else's. You decide whether to respond to e-mails in the middle of the night, whether to take the trip to Asia for a project, how long you stay on vacation and whether to turn off your phone. There's value in having flexibility, and it can result in a healthier lifestyle. More time for yourself and your family brings joy to most people.

As you can see, there are trade-offs, but it's best to have an awareness of how the business world is shifting in its workforce and where your career may be heading.

Chapter Endnotes

1   Deloitte. "The Alternative Workforce: It's Now Mainstream. 2019 Global Human Capital Trends". www2.deloitte.com. 2019. https://www2.deloitte.com/us/en/insights/focus/human-capital-trends/2019/alternative-workforce-gig-economy.html.
2   Frazer, John. "How the Gig Economy Is Reshaping Careers for the Next Generation". Forbes.com. February 25, 2019. https://www.forbes.com/sites/johnfrazer1/2019/02/15/how-the-gig-economy-is-reshaping-careers-for-the-next-generation/?sh=40bb5bd749ad.

CHAPTER 12

Planning for Financial Independence—The Math

Planning for retirement comes with mixed emotions. On one hand, there's bound to be excitement about sleeping in, missing the dreaded Monday morning commute, spending quality time with family, picking up new hobbies, and fulfilling a bucket list. On the other hand, there's anxiety about no longer receiving a paycheck and trying to make sure your hard-earned wealth lasts.

The most common retirement financial question is, "Do I have enough?" It's a simple question without a simple answer. After all, the math for retirement relies on many variables that are unknown ahead of time. You don't know how long your retirement will last. You don't know what health care costs you'll experience in retirement. You don't know what your investments will return, in what order those returns will occur, and what inflation will be.

With so many unknowns, it's important to build in some conservatism, analyze your situation several different ways, and seek counsel from those who have seen it all before. In this chapter, we'll provide some high-level guidance on how to determine whether you are financially ready to retire.

Goal Setting

The first step in determining retirement readiness is figuring out how much you plan to spend in retirement. There's a popular rule of thumb that says when you are retired, you'll spend about 70 to 80 percent of what you currently spend. Given our experience working with hundreds of retirees, we *do not* agree with this rule.

Each day in retirement is like a weekend, and most of us spend more money on weekends than on weekdays. Early in retirement, when you're unconfined by office life, you are likely to travel more, shop more, and spend more on hobbies. Spending typically, but not always, declines midway through retirement and then picks back up with high health care costs later in life. Think about the shape of a smile - the left and right ends of the smile are high, and it dips in the middle. We call it the retirement spending smile.

Your spending is likely to follow this trend, but you don't want your retirement projections to hinge on reducing expenses midway through retirement. That said, the key spending number we recommend using for planning purposes is what you expect to spend annually those first few years. To calculate this spending target, we recommend tracking your expenses while in the workforce and adding in some buffer for travel, new cars, home renovations, and other less regular expenses. For example, if you spend $10,000 per month now, you may want to budget for $12,000 per month in retirement.

You'll also need to incorporate taxes in your retirement plan calculations. Speak with your accountant to get a sense of how much annual tax you are likely to pay in retirement. Some states offer tax breaks for retirees. Most, if not all, of your retirement income will not be subject to FICA or Medicare tax. In addition, some of your retirement income may be tax-free depending upon how you saved during your working years.

A Simple Framework

Once you've determined how much you plan to spend in retirement and your estimated annual taxes, you'll want to calculate how much income you can expect without touching your investment assets. Sources of income will differ by person but may include Social Security, pensions, or rental real estate income. The remaining gap between expenses and outside sources of income is what your investment assets will need to cover.

The 4 percent rule is a general rule of thumb that can help you determine whether you have enough investment assets to cover this gap. However, it does not replace the benefits of ongoing planning and monitoring of your financial strategy, which is extremely important to ensure you'll continue to have enough investment assets.

This 4 percent rule is based on looking at historical US stock returns, bond returns, and inflation going back to 1926. In most thirty-year periods over that time, you could withdraw more than 4 percent and not run out of money. In the worst thirty-year period over that time, you could withdraw only 4 percent. If you withdrew more than 4 percent, you would run out of money before year thirty. This method states that you can withdraw 4 percent of your investment assets the first year of retirement, adjust that withdrawal amount each year for inflation, and not have to worry about running out of money over thirty years if you have a balanced investment portfolio. For example, if you have $1 million in investment assets allocated approximately 60 percent to stocks and 40 percent to bonds, you can withdrawal $40,000 in your first year of retirement. If inflation is 3 percent, your withdrawal in year 2 can be $41,200.

If you have longevity in your family, have retired early, or have a pension that won't increase for inflation over time, you may want to withdraw less than 4 percent to help plan for a retirement lasting longer than thirty years. If you expect to have a retirement that lasts less than thirty years, or if you have other inflation protected sources of income, you may be able to withdraw more than 4 percent. We have analyzed the historical data, and here are sample initial withdrawal rates for different time horizons.[1]

Length of Retirement	Initial Withdrawal Rate
40 years	3.75%
35 years	3.85%
30 years	4.00%
25 years	4.20%
20 years	4.65%

It is worth noting that these percentages are based on simulated historical data and do not incorporate your specific situation. All calculations assume you have a prudently diversified portfolio without too much tied up in one stock, you don't allow your investment accounts to get too far out of balance, you don't try to time the market, and there is no way to accurately predict the future.

Other Methods

The 4 percent rule is a starting framework for determining whether you have enough investment assets to retire. There are more sophisticated methods that are especially helpful for executives with stock options, deferred compensation, pensions, and complicated tax situations. These methods include Monte Carlo simulations that overlay your specific assets, sources of income, and expenses with potential investment returns and risks. We run these simulations for our clients leading up to retirement and during retirement to help ensure they remain on track for a financially secure future.

Regardless of the methodology you use to determine whether you have enough to retire, there is an ongoing question that must be addressed: Will it continue to be enough? We recommend reviewing your finances at least annually in retirement and ensuring your investment portfolio is carefully balanced with enough assets to grow and outpace inflation, yet it has a reasonable balance to safety and preservation to weather through bear markets. Making small, tactical shifts to your investment portfolio can not only help increase the life of your portfolio but can also alleviate the fear of missing out if you don't take any action during bull or bear markets. If you don't have the confidence to handle your investments yourself, hire a professional. If you do have the tools and knowledge, be sure to have a partner, family friend, or other objective set of eyes occasionally look at your overall well-being. Many don't like to share personal financial information with friends, but it's better than making a colossal financial mistake from which you can't recover.

Chapter Endnote

1   The analyses provided are for illustrative purposes only. They are not indicative of a particular client's situation. Past performance is not a guarantee of future results. Analyses were created using S&P 500, Russell 2000, US Intermediate Government Bonds, and CPI data. They assume a retirement period beginning in December 1968. The initial portfolio balance is assumed to be allocated 48 percent in US large cap stocks, 12 percent in US small cap stocks, and 40 percent in bonds and is rebalanced annually. Investors cannot invest directly in an unmanaged index.

CHAPTER 13

Experiencing a Financial Setback

Over the span of your lifetime, you will likely experience a dozen or more recessions and bear markets. Bear markets are common; there have been twenty-five of them since 1928.[1] When financial turmoil happens, it can feel unsettling. Seeing your 401(k) balance go backward is hard enough on its own, but when you add in fears about your health, income, career, or plans for retirement, it's easy to get overwhelmed by emotions and make impulsive decisions.

It's surprisingly hard to do nothing. Staying seated during a crisis goes against our human instincts. In our experience, people are almost never happy with the decisions they make in the middle of a crisis. So how can you be expected to sit still when financial uncertainty is staring you in the face? The following are disciplines to help you navigate through financial twists and turns.

> In our experience, people are almost never happy with the decisions they make in the middle of a crisis.

Focus on the Big Picture

Having a comprehensive financial plan in place before a storm strikes ensures you're ready when it inevitably comes. If you don't have a plan, talk with a professional about how to build one. If you do have a plan, during a financial setback is a great time to review your financial plan and determine whether it still suits your needs. You may be surprised how little your financial trajectory changes if you planned ahead for bad economic times.

Evaluate and Increase Your Cash Reserves

It's important to have plenty of cash in the bank to cover emergencies, job layoffs, or other unforeseen expenses while you are working. The closer you are to retirement, the more you should focus on building your cash reserves to equal one to three years of your living expenses. Not only will this give you comfort and flexibility to ride out a financial storm, but it also provides more confidence if you are knocking on retirement's door.

Generally speaking, it is not wise to sell your stocks when the market is down, because you will be selling positions that have temporarily declined in market value. If you are considering taking money out of your investments during a financial setback, first look to use cash to cover expenses during bear markets. Also, have enough invested in bonds to cover three or

> It is not wise to sell your stocks when the market is down

more years of expenses, thereby leaving your stock portfolio untouched even longer. These principles matter in retirement too.

For example, a retired couple needs $5,000 each month from their portfolio to supplement their pension and Social Security income. This couple should aim to have approximately $60,000–$180,000 in cash which could help cover expenses for a year or more if they need wait for a bear market to run its course.

Rerun Your Numbers

When a financial setback occurs close to your retirement date, it is normal to wonder whether you are still on track to meet your magic number for retirement. For those considering retiring in the near term, if your portfolio suddenly takes a hit, working longer or waiting for the stock market to rebound is certainly a consideration. Before you jump to conclusions, though, rerun the math. Most people who have a well-balanced, diversified portfolio can rely on their investments to carry them through a crisis.

The 4 Percent Rule Works in Many Market Conditions

The 4 percent rule has worked even through many periods of poor returns, including a few of the worst downturns in history: The Great Depression, the tech bubble, and the Great Recession. History shows that there is a low probability that a person or couple with a diversified portfolio will deplete their principal over thirty years if they enter retirement and withdraw no more than 4 percent of their beginning balance, adjusted for inflation each year.

Based on this 4 percent withdrawal principle, if you retire with $1 million this year—even though it may be down right now—you can still withdraw $40,000 (4 percent of $1 million) from your portfolio in year one. In year two, you can increase your withdrawal to $41,200 (assuming 3 percent inflation), and so on.

If you have probability analysis built into your financial plan, use this time to rerun those scenarios as another method for determining whether your retirement spending plans are still realistic.

Review and Adjust Your Investment Portfolio

Next, remember the stock market is volatile and bear markets are normal. Risk is the reason we get a return. But history has shown the longer you stay invested, the more likely you are to generate a positive return. Over the last ninety-one years of stock market history, stocks have been up 77 percent of the time.[1] The average decline for the S&P 500 index in a bear market is approximately 34 percent, and the average gain in a bull market is approximately 153 percent.[2] Over the last seventy years, approximately 75 percent of the S&P 500's strongest days have occurred during bear markets.[3] Right now we are still in the midst of the COVID-19 pandemic. Between March and April 2020, we had the fastest stock market drawdown in history—over 30 percent—followed by the best fifty trading days in the S&P 500 ever. If history has taught us anything, the best way to weather the storm is to stay the course because it is challenging to time the market bottom, and you cannot afford to miss out on the often quick recovery.

Every bear market is like this in a sense. It's never a straight line down with an all-clear sign at the bottom. The unwinding of the tech bubble in 2000–2002 was anything but smooth. On the way to the eventual bottom, there were four separate rallies of over 10 percent, including a spike of over 20 percent. There was also a 21 percent rally in the middle of the financial crisis in 2008, not to mention several other double-digit bounces.[2] It would be tough to make a case that any fundamentals or headlines gave investors a sign that the bear market was about to be over. The market tends to recover well in advance of the dust settling, but we can know that only after the fact.

> Every bear market is like this in a sense. It's never a straight line down with an all-clear sign at the bottom.

Here are other investment strategies to consider during a financial downturn.

- Review your investments and rebalance your portfolio. For example, if you had set 75 percent of your 401(k) to be invested in stock funds, a market correction may have reduced your stock allocation to 65 percent of your portfolio. Remember, you want to buy low and sell high. By rebalancing and bringing stocks back up to 75 percent, you will be able to buy more stocks at temporarily depressed prices.
- Review your monthly and annual savings goals, and make certain enough money is going into stocks. The percentage for stock investments will depend on various factors, such as your personal time frame for retirement, but keep in mind stocks have a good chance to grow over time.
- If you have fewer than five years until retirement, consider having at least 20–40 percent of your investment portfolio in bonds. The

percentage depends on how soon you plan to draw down on your portfolio and your risk tolerance.

- Consider increasing the percentage of pay going to your 401(k) contributions, especially if you are not already contributing the maximum amount every year.

- Do not move all of your investments to cash. If watching your investments decline causes you heartburn, it's better to move some money from stocks into bonds.

- If all or most of your portfolio is invested in your company stock, think carefully about this move. Your human capital is 100 percent tied to your company. Should your investments be too? In addition, any company match in your 401(k) may be made in company stock. Many executives and senior-level managers also have a lot of stock options or restricted stock grants, making them even more tied to the fortunes of their company.

Although it can be difficult to watch your portfolio fluctuate, it's important to keep in mind that downturns and financial setbacks are a temporary part of the financial process. If you can avoid letting emotions derail your investment and financial strategy, it should pay off when the market and economy recovers.

A special thanks to Brightworth senior investment analyst John Darby, CFA, for his contributions to this chapter.

Chapter Endnotes

1   Hartford Funds. "10 Things You Should Know About Bear Markets". 2020. https://www.hartfordfunds.com/practice-management/client-conversations/bear-markets.html.

2   Invesco. "Bull and Bear Markets—Historical Trends and Portfolio Impact". May, 2019. https://www.invesco.com/us-rest/contentdetail?contentId=049233173 f5c3510VgnVCM100000c2f1bf0aRCRD&audienceType=investors.

3   Charles Schwab. "When Markets Dip, Don't Drop Out". March 12, 2020. https://www.schwab.com/resource-center/insights/content/when-markets-dip-dont-drop-out.

CHAPTER 14

Preparing for Post Corporate Life— Mentally and Physically

Some corporate executives celebrate retirement as the beginning of the next chapter of their lives. Some mourn retirement as the end of an era. Almost all corporate executives we've worked with tell us retirement is something like jumping off a moving train.

> Retirement is something like jumping off a moving train.

A moving train has momentum. A moving train, like most executives, has taken significant time and has exerted significant energy to get to where it is, but when a successful, driven, and devoted executive retires, the hard truth is that the company train will keep chugging along. The company's next initiatives will continue full speed ahead as the retired executive is left to watch the train grow smaller and ever more distant.

It's important to proactively prepare for your jump off the train. You're going to want to slow it down as much as you can, hit the new ground as softly as you can, and stick the landing as best as you can.

Slowing It Down

Many of the people we've seen retire well have done a lot of the same things. First, they accept that the company can and will go on without them. As impossible as it may be to believe that someone else will be able to keep watch over what you have passionately guarded, there will be another person up to the task. Sure, they may not do it as well as you or in the same way you did it, but it's important to face the truth that a successful company is not going to let necessary responsibilities go undone or be carried out ineptly.

Second, they work with their manager to agree upon a retirement date that is far enough out to allow them to put a bow on any projects they want to see through to completion or make sure are in good enough shape for the baton to be successfully passed. Once the retirement date is agreed upon, they share it with their peers and subordinates as appropriate.

Every typical marker such as a personal development plan, an annual conference, or a company holiday party is a last, but at least everyone knows it, including the retiring executive. This can allow executives to experience great satisfaction in the completion of a major corporate objective they've been working on and great comfort and confidence with a successfully passed on responsibility. As the last markers pass off the calendar, they can be points of reflection and points of celebration. As the inevitable retirement date nears, the number of remaining objectives should be shrinking, and the number of batons to pass should be declining. If this technique is done successfully, winding down the year before retirement can afford executives the chance to tap the brakes a little from their historically breakneck corporate pace before they actually retire.

> Winding down the year before retirement can afford executives the chance to tap the brakes a little from their historically breakneck corporate pace before they actually retire.

Third, they help their peers and likely successors while they are still working. We've heard it said that a way to get promoted is to replace yourself. Perhaps it can also be said that one of the ways executives can slow things down and retire well is also to replace themselves. Many hours are shared with coworkers, and many battles in the trenches have been fought with them. They obviously need to know how to continue the fight without you, and as we've seen with many retiring executives, soon-to-be retirees may need the peace of mind knowing their soon-to-be former coworkers can continue the fight without them. The only way for both parties to know this is to let peers and successors try your responsibilities. As responsibilities are being shared or are decreasing, retiring executives should have a little more time on their hands and have a chance to slow down. Besides, isn't it better to be able to share your wisdom while you are still working than having panicked coworkers texting you or calling you on your first retired Monday?

> Isn't it better to be able to share your wisdom while you are still working than having panicked coworkers texting you or calling you on your first retired Monday?

Hitting the New Ground Softly

Unfortunately, we've seen far too many corporate executives crash into their new retirement ground. Sometimes it resembles an abrupt thud. Other times, especially if they haven't slowed down any, it's one painful, spiraling hit after another until the emotionally battered and bruised executive eventually comes to a stop. Most executives spend more time with their coworkers than they do with their families and their friends, and this can pose real problems in retirement.

First, not all work friends end up being close friends once the commonality of work is removed and the cadence of frequently seeing one another drastically declines. This can create a void.

Second, if executives have not kept up their relationship with their partners, their children, or their friends, having a drastic increase in the ability to spend time with these people can create unexpected experiences. It may quickly become apparent that there is not as much love, connectivity, or desire to be around one another as the executive had planned on. This can create a bigger void.

Third, if an executive's life was their career and their career was their life, there might not be a lot of hobbies. With drastically more free time, having everyday feel like a Saturday can quickly move from a blessing to a curse.

If a retired executive's work friendships quickly halt, current family and friend relationships aren't strong enough to fill a work week, and there are no real hobbies in place to speak of, then retirement can feel like the abrupt thud. If some work friendships temporarily remain, family and friend relationships briefly flare but then return to a steady

> With drastically more free time, having everyday feel like a Saturday can quickly move from a blessing to a curse.

flicker, and golf or tennis gets old really fast, retirement can feel like a medical monitor with a series of peaks and valleys as the executive keeps flipping over and over.

To avoid these traps, it is critical to make work friendships extend outside of work. Take the time to truly engage or reengage your partner, children, and friends before you retire. Make sure you know at least one thing you would like to do in your spare time that you can do alone. Other recommendations would include having a formally laid out bucket list for your first several months of retirement and to have a fully developed weekly schedule or daily routine for the time periods when you aren't working on the bucket list. What you don't want is boredom. This can lead to marital problems, family problems, sadness, depression, and believe it or not a desire to go back to work full-time. Take the time to explore what you are moving toward, not just what you are leaving behind.

Sticking the Landing

Anyone who watches the Olympics can tell you that no matter how good gymnasts' routines have been, if they don't stick the landing, their performance may not be remembered as being successful. The same holds true for corporate executives. No matter how good your career has been, if you don't stick the retirement landing, the last, bitter taste may cause you to view your career as unsuccessful.

> No matter how good your career has been, if you don't stick the retirement landing, the last, bitter taste may cause you to view your career as unsuccessful.

In a perfect world, most executives want to go out on their terms and on their timing. This may mean going out before you are told you need to (or have to). You don't have to retire when you are at the peak of your game, but you also want to make sure you aren't still trying to be the leading contributor when you are no longer able to do so. Retire with dignity and with grace.

We've talked about the importance of slowing down before you jump off the corporate train, but it's also good not to completely coast, even if you are able. You don't have to be the first to arrive at the office or the last one to leave. Rather, end with a regular, measured pace. Do everything you possibly can to leave things in good shape for your subordinates, your peers, your boss, and your company. If you do that, everyone will appreciate you and fondly remember you.

Even if you get all the financial considerations of retirement correct and you have plenty of money, if you get the softer side of retiring wrong, you will get retirement wrong. We do everything in our power to ensure that our retiring corporate executives end their careers well in the way of financial confidence, comfort, and clarity. Even so, we have seen far too many executives not retire well because they didn't slow down, they truly didn't know how they were going to land, and they didn't stick their landing.

> If you get the softer side of retiring wrong, you will get retirement wrong.

Retirement is undoubtedly the end of a chapter, but hopefully it's not the end of your book. With continuously rising life expectancies, retirement may be the beginning of the longest season of your life. Those who have retired well often passionately tell us that there is more to life than riding on the corporate train. In some cases, they've even discovered that riding on the corporate train wasn't all it was cracked up to be.

CHAPTER 15

Your Final Working Year and the Critical Years Between 59 ½ and 72

Hopefully by now you've addressed the "Do I have enough to retire?" question, and you have a sense of how you'll be occupying your time in the early years of retirement. Here are some other important items you'll want to make sure are buttoned up during your final working year.

Have a Retirement Healthcare and Long-Term Care Strategy in Place

Depending upon the company you are retiring from, you may be able to participate in their employer-provided retiree healthcare insurance coverage. If you are over the age of sixty-five, this will typically be secondary coverage to Medicare. Mark your calendar for three months prior to turning age sixty-five so you don't forget to sign up for Medicare in a timely manner. For those retiring past age sixty-five who have not enrolled in Medicare due to participating in the group health insurance plan, there is a special enrollment period beginning the month after employment ends, lasting for eight months. Failure to act within the special enrollment period can lead to significant penalties and costs.

For those not eligible for company-sponsored retiree coverage, you will need to find your own private coverage. Work with a qualified insurance advisor who can shop the marketplace to find you the best coverage at the best price, given your list of preferred doctors and required medications.

You may be entitled to COBRA coverage, which allows you to keep your prior group coverage in place for up to eighteen months. Although this can be an easy temporary solution, it is typically expensive because company subsidies no longer help defray the cost.

Next, if you don't already have long-term care insurance, consider how the purchase of a policy may protect or enhance your financial situation in retirement. Statistics suggest that at least one partner will need long-term care at some point in retirement. In fact, 52 percent of people turning age sixty-five will need long-term care services during their lifetime.[1] Depending on the level of care needed and duration, this can have a devastating effect on a retirement savings portfolio. Moreover, a common misconception is that Medicare or Medicare supplement insurance policies will provide coverage for this need. This is simply not true.

This is also a good time to assess your need for life insurance. If you have historically owned life insurance to replace your income, your needs may be different after retirement. Theoretically, you no longer have an insurance need for income replacement at retirement because you have accumulated enough assets. Some clients have switched the premiums they are paying for life insurance to premiums for long-term care insurance at this point in their lives.

Consider Paying Off Debt

One of the most frequently discussed topics when helping clients prepare for retirement is how to handle outstanding debt. Simple math can make the argument for keeping debt in place in retirement, particularly considering the low interest rate environment of the last decade. After all, if you can borrow money at 3 percent and earn 6 percent on your cash that remains invested, why not take advantage? However, eliminating the dark cloud of debt hanging overhead in retirement is one of the greatest sources of relief and peace of mind to clients, regardless of what the numbers say to do. In addition, minimizing your fixed monthly expenses is a key to providing maximum financial flexibility in retirement. A mortgage is often the household's largest fixed monthly expense.

A big part of financial independence is not owing anyone else money.

Simplify and Organize

As you wind down your professional career, now is a great time to simplify your financial life as well. After years of work and possibly stops at several different employers, you may have multiple investment accounts that can be consolidated. Merging these accounts can not only bring you peace of mind in knowing that things are less likely to slip through the cracks but also streamline the process of gathering documents at annual tax filing time. Less accounts equals fewer 1099 tax forms to keep up with. In the case of retirement accounts, this can also allow for easier calculations of your required minimum distributions after you reach age seventy-two. For former employer retirement plans such as 401(k)s, 403(b)s, or 457(b), be careful to select the rollover option when moving these accounts instead of a withdrawal, which is taxable as ordinary income to you.

Know Your Withdrawal Strategy

Map out what "buckets" your income is going to come from in retirement. This will be your new paycheck. For many corporate executives, their income, especially in the first few years of retirement, can feel lumpy. Stock options still to be exercised, restricted stock pays out, deferred compensation payments begin, and nonqualified retirement plans may pay in a one-time lump sum shortly after leaving the company. Pension payments may also come into play. With all this lumpiness, we've found some clients prefer to park all these payments in their savings or investment account and have a regular, monthly withdrawal from those accounts that goes into their checking account. Others stockpile the cash and draw down from it as they need, which can allow your other investment accounts to grow and defer paying taxes, for example, on 401(k) distributions that don't need to begin until age seventy-two.

Net Unrealized Appreciation

As discussed in this book's 401(k) chapter, if you have accumulated a significant amount of company stock within your company retirement plan over many years, you may benefit from net unrealized appreciation (NUA), depending on your cost basis in those company shares. Under the right scenario, you could save thousands of dollars in tax by transferring some or all your company stock to a brokerage account at retirement. This is a sophisticated tax strategy and should be evaluated by a competent advisor prior to diversifying out of company stock or rolling over your retirement plan to another retirement account. Nail this down during your final working year.

Review Your Deferred Compensation Account

If you have had the opportunity to contribute income to a deferred compensation retirement plan, spend time reviewing your balances and elections. For each year you deferred income into this plan, you likely selected a payout schedule upon separation from service at the company. This payout could be one lump sum after retirement, or it could be over a period such as five or ten years. Map out these various distributions because this can have a significant effect on your year-to-year cash flow in retirement.

In retrospect, if you now find that some of your elections for deferred compensation payments are less than ideal, some company plans may allow you to make changes, but these are typically required at least twelve months before separation from service, so it is critical that this be addressed early in your retirement preparations. While you are reviewing deferred compensation, also ensure that you have an appropriately diversified investment allocation as you are heading into retirement.

Know How Your Long-Term Incentive Plans Carry into Retirement, or Not

It's likely that you have long-term incentive compensation that will carry over into the first several years of your retirement. This is very common with stock option and restricted stock awards. Understand when these awards pay out in retirement, and whether you will forfeit any of them based on your retirement date.

In the case of stock options, you want to be clear on the time frame remaining to exercise your options. Have a strategy to map this out with your overall cashflow needs, taxes, and most important your ability to meet your goals. Again, these can represent a significant portion of your net worth and overall financial well-being.

Plan Your Charitable Giving

Depending on the time of year you retire, it is possible that your last year of working is your largest income year, but it could be the year after. This is often due to distributions of deferred compensation accounts, automatic vesting of restricted stock, severance payments, nonqualified retirement plan payouts, and other income items at retirement. In a large income year, any available tax deductions become increasingly valuable. Consequently, if you are charitably inclined, consider deferring or accelerating charitable giving to a higher income year, if possible.

We often help clients gift several years' worth of annual giving to a donor advised fund in the year they retire. For more information, read chapter 5.

Pension Puzzle

If you qualify for a company pension benefit, determine the payout options available to you and start thinking through which option will be the best fit. This can be the single most important decision you make regarding your retirement, and it should be carefully thought through. You'll be making an irrevocable election on your pension paperwork.

During your final year, request updated pension benefit projections from your benefits department based on your intended retirement date and pension benefit commencement date.

Determine When to File for Social Security Benefits

Social Security benefits play an important role in retirement calculations. There are several factors that go into answering the question "When should I file for Social Security?" Generally, the longer you wait to start taking your benefits, the higher your benefit will be. The earliest you can start to receive Social Security retirement benefits is age sixty-two. Delayed retirement is age seventy. Full retirement age—when your benefits will not be reduced by taking them early—is based on your year of birth, but for most people reading this book, it will be sixty-six or sixty-seven.

If you plan to consult or work part-time during the early years of retirement, it's best to postpone taking Social Security until at least your full retirement age. The reason is there is an annual earned income limitation whereby your Social Security benefits will be reduced if you make over a certain earned income threshold. For 2021, that earnings limit is $18,960.

It is important to note whether you have nonqualified stock options carrying into retirement. If you exercise these options while under your full retirement age, the income reported on tax form W-2 will appear as earned income to the Social Security Administration. If you are taking Social Security benefits early, they may flag your benefits as needing to be reduced or paid back because you made too much money. However, stock options are a form of deferred compensation when exercised in retirement, and they do not impact your Social Security benefits. If you get a notice from Social Security saying otherwise, contact your local Social Security office and bring form ssa-131 (which needs to be filled out by your former employer) clarifying your stock option income was not earned income.

Next, if you do not have any income from consulting or part-time work, or long-term incentives paying out the early years of retirement, that could be an argument for taking benefits early. It's better to have Social Security benefits coming into your bank account to help pay your bills each month in retirement, versus taking money out of your investment portfolio to pay those same bills. Also, nobody knows how long one will live, so if you have health issues, that's another argument to taking benefits early.

Finally, be sure to review your wage history on your Social Security statement to ensure its accuracy before you start electing benefits. If there's a discrepancy, it will take some time to resolve it, so address this in your final working year.

If you have any questions or concerns about your Social Security strategy, work with a financial professional to help you run the numbers while weighing the qualitative aspects of the equation such as health, desire to work part-time, and survivor needs.

Buy a New Car, Address Home Repairs

Large expenses such as home repairs or buying a new car feel much better to tackle while you still have a paycheck coming in. It can be a bit more unsettling to write these large checks early in retirement when you are still adjusting to life without a steady paycheck. We recommend clients think through any large expenses they may want to incur, or need to incur, in the next few years and set aside the cash before retiring.

Your final year of work will come and go quickly. Careful preparation before your final day can go a long way towards making the adjustment a smooth one.

Chapter Endnote

1   Benz, Christine. "Must Know Statistics About Long-Term Care, 2019 Edition". *Morningstar.com*, November 25, 2019. https://www.morningstar.com/articles/957487/must-know-statistics-about-long-term-care-2019-edition.

CHAPTER 16

Do It Yourself, or Hire Professionals

We've covered a lot of ground with your personal finances in this book. After reading this book, if you've found yourself more educated, with elevated confidence and optimism about your future, we consider that a success.

If you are overwhelmed, don't be. There is a lot of thought and detail that goes into financial strategies, and financial planning is a lifelong process. Start small, make incremental improvements, and over time that will lead to better financial outcomes.

In addition to this book, there are two other routes to help you address your financial strategy. The first is hiring a professional to partner with you through your life's financial journey. The second option is handling it yourself.

Starting with the second option, there are several online and technological resources available to corporate executives to help build and preserve wealth. Many employers offer online tools through the 401(k) website. Some banks and investment custodial firms offer online financial planning tools when you open a bank or investment account there, where you can calculate how much you need to save for retirement, inputting certain basic assumptions such as your age, retirement date, desired living expenses in retirement, and current assets. With these online tools their inputs may be limited to the data in their system and may not have the capability for you to enter external information. For example, your 401(k) provider has your 401(k) balance, but does it ask for your partner's 401(k) balance for retirement calculations? Does the software ask for a specific Social Security estimate based on your personal work history, or does it estimate one for you? There are some other important details the general online calculators or software tools may not cover. Does it account for buying a new car every few years in retirement, or does it only ask you what your living expenses are today? Does it factor in when you will pay off your mortgage, which could drastically reduce your expense needs? What about long-term care and healthcare expenses? How about wedding expenses for your children? While these general online tools are wonderful for helping to give most people a base level of direction and understanding about how well they are positioned for retirement, they are not personal to you. You can't customize an online tool to address your specific situation.

Next, you may look to family, friends, and colleagues for advice to learn what they are doing or what hasn't worked. There is a level of trust people give their friends and loved ones when it comes to money advice, but at the same time, many people are not comfortable sharing their personal financial details with close contacts. Even those who seem financially successful may be living under a pile of debt, so in reality they are not good candidates to get advice from. Tread carefully when it comes to friends and family, whether asking for advice or giving it. Money is emotional, and if something goes wrong, you don't want personal relationships ruined.

Hiring a financial professional is another option if you need help with your finances. Caring for your money is like maintaining a luxury car: Do you take it to the corner autobody shop for the quick and inexpensive service, passing time in the dusty, small waiting area, or do you take your luxury car to the dealership so the experts can perform the maintenance while you drive away in a new loaner vehicle and get on with your daily agenda? For some people, the quick and inexpensive route fits their personality, and they don't see value in paying more for a specialist. But with all of life's priorities you are juggling, do you have enough time to pay attention to your money and make the maneuvers necessary to achieve your financial goals? Will you do something silly that could one day ruin all you've worked hard to build? A financial professional can be a sounding board and ideally becomes a trusted relationship that you look to for financial guidance. This can save you a tremendous amount of time as you don't need to figure it all out yourself; you have a human being to talk to (rather than a computer screen), and your family knows who to call in the event you are not around.

For senior corporate executives, your employer may provide a stipend to cover personal financial planning, legal, and tax advice from financial professionals, so be sure to take advantage of that perk if it's available to you.

If you are thinking of hiring a financial advisor, the following is from a white paper we wrote to help people understand the different types of advisors that exist, how their fees work, and other considerations and questions when interviewing a financial advisor:

Be Smart about Selecting a Financial Advisor

As the saying goes, "When times are good, anyone can make money." The eleven-year bull market following the Great Recession found stocks ending 2019 at all-time highs, but recent volatility has some investors uncertain on where the markets will go from here. Many are reevaluating their relationship with their financial advisor to ensure that they are in good hands.

At a time like this, some do-it-yourselfers may realize that they also want help. But how will you know if you are receiving good advice? Partnering with an advisor to guide you through the complexities of your financial strategy is an important decision that should not be taken lightly. Advisors differ greatly in terms of qualifications, compensation, and conflicts of interest. Also critical are the investment process and performance, which are the cornerstone of your financial strategy and key to your long-term success.

Qualifications

The financial services industry is diverse, and there are "advisors" from many types of firms—registered investment advisory firms (RIAs), banks, brokerage firms, insurance companies, CPA firms—who are in the business of helping people with their finances. Competent professionals may be found in any of these environments, but the scope of services varies widely, and it is important that the background and experience level of the advisor match the services being provided.

Services may range from the purchase of investment products (such as a stock, bond, mutual fund, annuity, or insurance policy) to comprehensive financial planning and fee-only investment management. Start by viewing a bio on the advisor's website (or request one directly) to review the advisor's educational background and years of experience. There are many designations in the financial industry, but some highly respected designations are the Certified Financial Planner (CFP) for financial planners, Chartered Financial Analyst (CFA) and Certified Investment Management Analyst (CIMA) for investment managers, and the Chartered Life Underwriter (CLU) for life insurance specialists.

There are services available online that help consumers learn more about financial advisors. FINRA has a broker check system (brokercheck.finra.org) that allows viewers to see where an advisor is registered and to view licenses, examinations, work history, criminal record, and regulatory background. For advisors of RIA firms (which includes fee firms), use the SEC's Investment Advisor Public Disclosure website (adviserinfo.sec.gov) to view the firm's ADV Part 1, which includes an overview of the firm, the types of clients the advisor works with, and any disciplinary history of the firm and its advisors, if applicable. It also includes a link to the firm's ADV Part 2 which details the firms' fees, services, and potential conflicts of interest. You may also wish to request a copy of the ADV 2b biographies directly from the firm. The ADV

2b provides information on each advisor's education, licenses, designations, and other credentials. The newly implemented ADV Part 3 can also be found on the adviserinfo.sec.gov website. It is a two-page, plain-English document intended to be used to review a firm's fees, services, account minimums, conflicts of interests, and disciplinary history, if applicable. It provides a quick overview of the firm, as well as conversation starter questions to ask the advisor. You may also consider asking the advisor for existing client references to learn more about the level of satisfaction, the customer experience, and how the advisor communicates with clients.

Compensation

Getting a clear picture of how an advisor gets paid is a critical part of the due diligence process. On one end of the spectrum, some advisors receive a commission when an investment or insurance product is sold. On the other end, fee-only advisors may be paid a stated fee (flat rate, hourly rate, or a percentage of assets under management) by their clients in exchange for services.

A huge middle ground also exists between these two models called fee-based compensation. Fee-based advisors have the ability to accept both stated fees and commissions, so steering through the formal relationship to understand which capacity the advisor is serving under is often confusing. Regardless of the method, it is important to know what you are paying, so be sure to ask the advisor for a detailed listing of commissions for each product or a fee schedule in writing.

Conflicts of Interest

Another key point to understand is how incentives are aligned for an advisor so that you can properly evaluate any potential conflicts of interest. One such example is with the recommendation of investment or insurance products. Some firms create proprietary products which they offer to clients, whereas firms with an "open architecture" have the ability to offer products created by another firm in addition to their own proprietary products (if they have them). Investments can vary widely with different characteristics such as structure, investment style, expenses, and performance, but some advisors are paid a higher commission to sell the proprietary investment products of their own firm. Other considerations include who else might be getting paid, because there are sometimes monetary kickbacks from referrals, money managers, or clearing houses where trades are placed. (Brightworth is a fee-only firm and receives no compensation from third-party money managers or clearing houses.)

Investment Process and Performance

Your investment portfolio is the cornerstone of your financial strategy, and your advisor's investment philosophy and process will be a major determinant of its success. You will also need the proper accountability and reporting to maintain trust in your advisor over time. The following are some questions worth asking.

Philosophy

"Does your investment approach depend upon market timing, trading strategies, or do you believe in buy-and-hold, long-term investing?"

"Do you take a passive or active approach to investing?" Passive investors believe the markets are efficient and invest in broad market indexes, whereas active managers attempt to find opportunities they believe will have higher returns than the indexes.

"What is your investment strategy, and how does it drive the strategic and tactical asset allocation of the portfolio?"

Process

"How will my asset allocation and investment mix be determined?" Make sure that financial goals, investment risk tolerance, time horizon, and tax situation are discussed before the funds are invested.

"Will you articulate the investment objectives for my portfolio in writing (usually in the form of an investment policy statement)?"

"Where are the funds custodied?" Be sure that the proper checks and balances are in place and that you never transfer assets to someone other than an independent, third-party custodian such as Charles Schwab or Fidelity. Make sure that you receive a periodic statement directly from the custodian.

"How are investment decisions made? Do you make decisions on your own, or is there a team that makes investment decisions?"

"What is the process for ongoing monitoring and adjustments to the portfolio as market conditions change?"

"How will the management of my portfolio change when I start taking withdrawals?"

"How often are the portfolios rebalanced?"

Investment Performance and Accountability

Once you engage an advisor, it is important that there is total disclosure and accountability. Make sure that you receive regular and timely performance data for your investment portfolio on an ongoing basis so that you know how your portfolio has done as compared to relevant indices. It is important that the performance data is time weighted, which reflects the true performance of the investments and is not skewed by the timing of deposits and withdrawals into the portfolio. If your returns are unrealistically consistent year after year as market conditions change, take note because this could be a red flag for fraud.

Long-Term Approach

It may take many years to fully capture the rewards of a solid long-term financial planning and investment strategy. A financial strategy continues to evolve over time as factors such as client situations, markets, and tax laws change, but it is very important to have a consistent strategy in place. A relationship with an advisor is intended to be long term, and it is important that you find a trustworthy individual to partner with for many years. When evaluating your situation, take into account the stability of the firm and the advisor's longevity with the firm. With smaller independent firms, be sure to inquire as to whether they have a business succession plan in place. For many, it is important to know that there will be someone who knows you and your situation and can help your family over the long term.

The decision to work with an advisor should not be taken lightly, and there are many factors that should be considered in the due diligence process. In the end, however, successful relationships must be built on trust, which is the primary element that you must decide for yourself.

CHAPTER 17

Top Ten Takeaways

1. **Timing Is Everything**
   Address your finances now. The earlier you start planning, the better off your future will be.

2. **Save First**
   Make it a priority to put the maximum amount allowed into your 401(k) plan every year. Don't own too much company stock in your 401(k)—your livelihood and your personal investments should not be 100 percent tied to one company.

3. **Liquidity Is Key**
   Cash is key to financial flexibility. Keep three to twelve months of your living expenses in cash savings, and boost that amount if you think your company will go through a reorganization in the near future, your job may be at risk, or retirement is right around the corner.

4. **Maintain a Long-Term View**
   Keep your lifestyle in check as you make more money and climb the corporate ladder. The key to financial success is to spend less than you make and save the difference wisely over a long period of time.

5. **Know Your Employer's Stock Plan Details**
   Understand how your long-term incentive plans work, and have a plan to maximize the value and minimize your taxes. Stock options and restricted stock can become the largest components of your balance sheet over time and must be carefully managed. If you need expert advice, then hire tax, financial, and legal professionals who have a deep understanding of executive compensation.

6. **Insure High Impact Events**
   Cover yourself and your family with the right type and amount of insurance, especially early in your career. Your ability to earn a paycheck could be your family's largest financial asset for decades, and it must be protected.

7. **Plan Your Legacy**
   Have an updated estate plan. Make this a priority and review it with a lawyer every three to five years.

8. **Calculate What You Are Leaving on the Table**
   Should you leave your company voluntarily or involuntarily, understand how your company compensation and benefits rules change based on when and how you exit. Understand the assets you take with you versus those you forfeit.

9. **Jumping Off**
   If you plan well, you can retire early or have the flexibility to jump off the hamster wheel if you get burned out. Working long hours and carrying bundles of stress takes a toll, and tomorrow is not promised to anyone.

10. **Your Finish Line**
    Know the math behind "How much is enough to retire?", get expert advice, and plan for your next chapter. It's not what you are leaving behind; rather, it's what you are heading toward. Stick the landing. Retire with dignity and grace.

ABOUT THE AUTHORS

The wealth advisors at Brightworth have decades of experience providing financial advice to corporate executives working at iconic companies like[1]:

- Coca-Cola
- The Home Depot
- Amazon
- Nike
- UPS
- Macy's
- Delta Airlines, Inc.
- McDonalds
- Chick-fil-A
- GM
- Chevron
- Publix

We've seen some executives thrive financially, and some who've made bad decisions and failed at their finances. This book combines decades of wisdom from our wealth advisors, who wrote it to help you succeed in your career and with your money[2].

Dave Polstra   Lisa Brown   Ryan Halpern   Tom Presley

Bud Boland   Josh Monroe   Wesley Wood   Brett Covert

Chapter Endnotes

1   Brightworth has worked with clients who are either current or former employees of the above listed companies and/or their predecessors. This is not intended to imply that Brightworth is endorsed by the companies themselves.

2   Photographs of authors used with permission from Eric Bern (Headshot Studio Atlanta, an Eric Bern Studio Production), Kim Hummel (Kim Hummel Photography), and Rick Weissinger.